Devoted to God's Church

Core Values for Christian Fellowship

Sinclair B. Ferguson

THE BANNER OF TRUTH TRUST

THE BANNER OF TRUTH TRUST

Head Office
3 Murrayfield Road
Edinburgh
EH12 6EL
UK

North America Office
PO Box 621
Carlisle
PA 17013
USA

banneroftruth.org

First published 2020
© Sinclair B. Ferguson 2020
Reprinted 2021 (special)

*

ISBN
Print: 978 1 84871 976 7
EPUB: 978 1 84871 977 4
Kindle: 978 1 84871 978 1

*

Typeset in 11/15 pt Adobe Garamond Pro at
The Banner of Truth Trust, Edinburgh

Printed in the USA by
Versa Press Inc.,
East Peoria, IL.

WITH GRATITUDE

TO

THE 'ORDINARY' CHRISTIANS

WHO

SHOWED ME CHRIST

NURTURED ME IN THE FAITH

PRAYED FOR ME REGULARLY

ENCOURAGED ME IN THE MINISTRY

AND

TAUGHT ME TO LOVE THE CHURCH

Contents

Introduction

———

There are already many excellent books about the church. Recent decades have witnessed an exponential growth of titles on the subject. This is for at least two reasons. The first is the *decline* of the church in the West, raising the question 'What are we to do?' The second, paradoxically, is the *growth* of certain churches (often enough to 'mega-church size'). Thus ministers, pastors and church leaders who have 'succeeded' share their secrets with others. We all gravitate towards success.

Probably most of these books are of particular interest to those who *lead* churches and shape their life (or to those who would like to be leaders so that they could *change* their church!). They outline what our churches should be and sometimes describe how the author's church grew to become what it is and, at least by implication, how your church can follow in its footsteps.

This is not that kind of book. It certainly does not promise success if only a certain model is followed. No doubt it has been influenced by the churches in which I have served. But it is meant for a wider readership. Its focus is on what it means for Christians to be members of a church. After all, *we are the church*. So it is not a book full of ideas about how your church ought to change or what it needs to do in order to grow or to be successful. Rather it is about how we fit in to our own church, given that each church has a unique location and a unique composition of members. It tries to unfold some basic principles that are applicable to every Christian and to any congregation. It is, as the sub-title suggests, a book about our core values as Christians who belong to the family of God.

I hope these pages will also be helpful to people on the periphery of churches, wondering about what it means to belong to one, perhaps even considering membership in one. In fact, these pages were 'birthed' in my mind by the question: 'What book would I recommend to someone who was thinking about membership in *our church*?' The truth is, each church is so unique that probably every church needs to write its own book! Yet, at the same time, there are hallmarks of church life that should be stamped on all of our churches because they are applicable everywhere and anywhere. There are core values in the New Testament for any size of church, in any part of the world, at any time. No matter what our distinctive views on church government, on baptism, or precisely how we celebrate the Lord's Supper, the core biblical teaching remains the same for all of us. And my own conviction is that for most Christians these core values—not so much the distinctive elements in our forms of government, denominational connections or the like—are what really matters on a day to day and week to week basis.

So *Devoted to God's Church* has the goal of serving all shapes and sizes of church, not to hold up one kind of church as the model. At the end of the day we need to remember that 'Christ loved the church and gave himself up for her' (Eph. 5:25) applies not only to the entire church but to our congregation as well. And that being the case, we should follow his example. We need to be delivered from the myth that 'If only I were a member of *that* church instead of *this* one I would become a much better and more faithful member.'

For these reasons, I hope that it might be possible to answer the question that prompted these pages ('What book would I recommend to someone who was thinking about membership in *our church*?') by saying, 'Well, you could start with *Devoted to God's Church*—it covers most of the bases of our church life here—and then, if you wanted to, we could talk later about how all this applies here in our own congregation.' These pages provide a modest tool, but I pray they may have the effect of recalibrating your commitment to Christ and love for the specific church family to which you belong.

Sinclair B. Ferguson
January, 2020

1

Family Life

or

What Is a Church?

———

Being a Christian involves *believing*: 'If you confess with your mouth that Jesus is Lord and believe in your heart that God raised him from the dead, you will be saved' (Rom. 10:9). But being a Christian is not an individualistic or isolationist activity. *Believing* also involves *belonging*. When the shepherd calls his sheep to him they inevitably come nearer to each other. When you come to Christ you are at the same time drawn nearer to others who have come to him. Being a Christian, by definition, involves belonging to the church—and that, in turn, means belonging to a particular church.

People have very different ideas of what that means and of how important—or otherwise—it is. In the New Testament however, two emphases are crystal clear: (1) belonging to the church is one of the privileges of being a Christian, and (2) it is also one of our central responsibilities. Belonging to a church family is not an optional extra.

People often have very definite, and sometimes very different, expectations about what is involved in belonging to a church.

Let me illustrate. When someone becomes a 'member' of a church there is usually some kind of process to go through.

It may be superficial. I remember hearing from a real estate agent that many colleagues in her particular city simply asked their house-searching clients what church they would like to join, and then passed on their names to that congregation. One could almost imagine the advertisement: 'Buy a House with Us—Includes Church Membership.'

Hopefully the reality of the situation was different from its appearance. And happily, the pathway to membership is usually more distinctively Christian than that! But even so, prospective church members come with very varied views on what church membership entails. They may (and do!) ask such revealing questions as:

- 'Do I give you my bank account number now?'

- 'I am living with my girlfriend … that's ok, isn't it?'

- 'I plan to come to the services from time to time; presumably that's fine?'

Which, if any, of these questioners would you expect to make headway in living the Christian life with a clear understanding of New Testament discipleship?

Have you ever checked out membership in Rotary International? Most towns or areas have a group; many cities have several. Their Constitution has an entire page on the subject of 'Attendance' alone![1] Yet, for all the privileges of membership in Rotary International and the corresponding responsibilities, these surely pale by comparison with the greater privileges of being a Christian and a member of the body of Christ. Should we not therefore expect that the responsibilities would be correspondingly greater? Yet, curiously, to spell out these responsibilities is sometimes to be accused of 'legalism' or to be described in similar pejorative terms—an accusation rarely if ever

---

[1] Given how casually we sometimes think about being a church member, it is worth knowing how seriously Rotary International takes membership! See Appendix at the end of this chapter.

levelled against Rotary International! Why would we expect a lower view of membership in the church of Jesus Christ than of membership in Rotary International?

So, let's begin at the beginning.

Whose church?

People are usually very surprised to learn that in the first half of the New Testament—the four Gospels of Matthew, Mark, Luke and John—there are only two passages in which the word 'church' is used. Can it therefore be all that important?

On both occasions the word is found on the lips of Jesus. The first is in Matthew 16:18:

> And I tell you, you are Peter, and on this rock *I will build my church*, and the gates of hell shall not prevail against it.

The second is in Matthew 18:15-17:

> If your brother sins against you, go and tell him his fault, between you and him alone. If he listens to you, you have gained your brother. But if he does not listen, take one or two others along with you, that every charge may be established by the evidence of two or three witnesses. If he refuses to listen to them, *tell it to the church*. And if he refuses to listen *even to the church*, let him be to you as a Gentile and a tax collector.

Nobody else in the gospel narrative uses the term.

Yet the church was absolutely central to the vision of Jesus. You can tell from the language in Matthew 16:18 that Jesus was making a statement of tremendous significance. He is outlining his mission and describing what he is planning to accomplish. He came to build his church. He has already begun to do it; he is continuing to do it; one day he will complete it.

We should not make the elementary mistake of thinking that the significance of an idea is to be judged exclusively by the number of times a person uses a particular expression to describe it. Jesus' words here have a programmatic ring. He is announcing his manifesto: '*I tell you … I will build* my church.'

Paul later emphasized the importance of the church to Jesus when he made the staggering claim that he governs the entire cosmos with a view to the well-being of the church (Eph. 1:22). Later in the same letter (which has a great deal to say about the church) he describes the way husbands should love their wives—'as Christ loved the church and gave himself for her …' (Eph. 5:25). The church is *that* important to the Saviour: he loved her and he died for her.

So, even although the word 'church' appears infrequently in the Gospels, there is no doubt that the church itself is of central importance. Christ rules the world for it. It is so important to him, so central in his purposes, so much the object of his love and affection, that he was willing to die for it:

> From heaven he came and sought her
> To be his holy bride
> With his own blood he bought her
> And for her life he died.[1]

If that is true, then it follows that as a disciple of Jesus I too should love the church. It should become central to my life. It is simply not possible to live a God-centred, Christ-centred, Spirit-led life unless my life is also church-centred. Unless, of course, I find myself stranded, Robinson Crusoe like, on a deserted island. Even so I would depend on my church at home to pray for me!

Anything that is of central importance to the Lord Jesus Christ must also be central to the Christian.

So, as we think about our own core values it is worthwhile taking stock and asking ourselves: To what extent am I a church-centred Christian? And do I think of the church as 'mine'—or as Christ's?

---

[1] From the hymn by Samuel John Stone (1839–1900), 'The Church's one foundation.'

Church at the centre

Each of us lives in a series of concentric spheres. Most of us have our roots in a family life. We also have a vocation in life that usually takes us out of our home and family context for many hours each week. Then we are also citizens and have specific privileges and responsibilities in relation to people around us in the context of society. And then, if we are Christians, there is the church. How are these life-spheres related to one another in a well-ordered Christian life?

That is a major point of discussion. But even the texts we have mentioned already suggest that for Christians the church is central. It is not an added extra—the icing on the cake of 'a good life well lived.' Rather, our life in the church lends its atmosphere to our social life; it energizes us in our vocational life to be salt and light in the world; and it is a basic dimension of, not merely an optional add-on to, our family life. In fact from one point of view the church is so central to the New Testament's vision of the Christian life that in some senses it is even more basic than the most basic of these other spheres, family life.

We need to think about this carefully, and its significance may well dawn on us only slowly. But it is the logical implication of at least three of Jesus' hardest sayings.

> (1) Whoever loves father or mother more than me is not worthy of me, and whoever loves son or daughter more than me is not worthy of me. (Matt. 10:37)

Here Jesus sets our ultimate priorities. He comes first. If that is the case, then his family has a certain kind of priority over my own family. Of course, by God's grace, my family life is meant to 'fit in' wonderfully with the purposes of Jesus. But the priority is not negotiable. If push comes to shove, Christ and his people come first.

Again Jesus said:

(2) For in the resurrection they neither marry nor are given in marriage, but are like angels in heaven. (Matt. 22:30)

The implication here is startling. Marriage and family relationships are, apparently, temporary. For all the wonder, potential joy and blessing of natural family life, its precise structures were never intended to last forever. One day our family relationships will be completely folded into the family of God. We should therefore be engaged in that process here and now.

Our Lord himself lived by this principle. He had a nuclear family—by the time of his public ministry consisting only of his mother Mary and his fairly numerous brothers and sisters. Yet for him 'church' came first. So, on one occasion when his family had come to see him, perhaps worried about the impact of his teaching and preaching, and fearing where it all might lead—and end—he responded with these strong words:

(3) And stretching out his hand toward his disciples, he said, 'Here are my mother and my brothers! For whoever does the will of my Father in heaven is my brother and sister and mother.' (Matt. 12:49, 50)

Lest we dodge the full force of his statement by suggesting that, since Jesus was the Son of God (and without a mother) he was an exception, we should remember that Mary really was his mother (Joseph of course was his adopting, not his natural father).

Thus, in these three statements in the Gospel that is often described specifically as 'The Disciples' Gospel' (the Gospel according to Matthew) we are taught how supremely important the church really is.

This perspective may be new to us, hard to swallow, more radical than we bargained for—the church given priority? Church more durable than family? This is not how we imagined Christianity!

But this would be to miss a very important emphasis in Jesus' teaching. So long as we give absolute priority to anything rather than to Christ we can never enjoy it as Christ intends us to. We mar the good when we prefer it to the better, because we thus forfeit the best. This principle includes our attitude to our family. When our own ambitions are aligned to those of Jesus, we will discover blessings in family life that we scarcely knew existed.

But there is another reason this is true. My family needs the church family for its own growth and health. No single family possesses all the resources it needs to be a truly and fully Christian family. We need support, friendship, example, wise counsel and much else from the church family. Two Christian parents are not in themselves adequate to rear one child for Christ—*they were never meant to be*. So the resources of our own family—no matter how wonderful—are scarcely adequate. We—and perhaps especially our children—need the church, and in that context we will be blessed beyond our expectation.

Here is a simple illustration. Years ago, in the church to which we belonged, one of our sons visited us over a weekend. After the evening service I saw him sitting at the back of the church talking to an elderly lady. She spoke to me the following week. She was a woman of relatively little education and very modest means; our son was a young surgeon. She did not mingle in social circles with surgeons or the like, and was scarcely able to contain her appreciation that he had noticed her and had spent time with her. Imagine the pleasure it gave me as a father (as well as her minister) to remind her of how in the past she had spoken to him and encouraged him at the end of evening worship when he was just a little boy! He had not forgotten her interest in him or her encouragement. It was 'natural' for him to want to speak to her. She had given him what we could not—the loving concern of an elderly Christian woman most of whose life had been lived with few resources and opportunities. No wonder then that, in a living church, family situations like this arise that prompt us to say 'This is why I love our church!'

It is in the context of such blessings that we need to learn to ask, *not*: 'How is church life to be fitted into my plans (for myself or my family)?' *but*: 'How do we fold our lives into the life of the church?'

All this becomes clearer when we grasp a basic principle. The church is the community in which the kingdom of Christ comes to expression; it is not a democracy run by elected representatives in which we debate priorities. It is Jesus' kingdom. So the first question that matters is: 'What is the will of the Lord Jesus?' Nor is the answer impossibly difficult. It is found in a relatively short—perhaps 250-page—book called *The New Testament*, a surprising amount of which is about life in the church. If only we would see that, it would both simplify and transform so much of our attitude to the church. In fact it would transform many churches!

What is the church?

One New Testament scholar has listed almost a hundred different metaphors for the church.[1] While a cursory glance at his list suggests that the number has been stretched as far as possible, it is still an impressive array and indicates how multi-dimensional the New Testament picture of the church is. But if we begin at the beginning, with our Lord's words, two pictures seem to be basic.

The city of God

Jesus is the church builder. This is implied in his words 'On this rock *I will build* my church and the gates of hell shall not prevail against it' (Matt. 16:18). Exactly what Jesus means here by 'hell' or in Greek '*Hades*' has been much discussed. *Hades* refers to the realm of the dead. Perhaps he had martyrdom in mind—a reality a number of the apostles would face.

[1] Paul S. Minear, *Images of the Church in the New Testament* (Cambridge: Lutterworth Press, 1960).

But perhaps the reference is more broadly to the organized powers of darkness. For Jesus speaks specifically about '*the gates* of hell.'

In the biblical world, cities were often walled round and therefore had 'gates.' These not only functioned as access and exit points, but also served as the location where policy was decided and justice administered by the city elders. Thus the husband of the 'excellent wife' in Proverbs 31:10-31 'is known in the gates when he sits among the elders of the land' (Prov. 31:23). Earlier in Israel's history, in the Book of Ruth, when Boaz decided he wanted to marry Ruth but realized she had a closer relative who might want to do so, he went to the Bethlehem city gate so that the whole issue could be decided before the elders of the city council 'legally' as it were (Ruth 4:1-12).

Jesus promises that 'the gates of hell' will not prevail against his church. The policies and plans adopted in the city of darkness will not prevail over the city of God! Jesus is building in enemy-occupied territory—a world over which Satan had become ruler (John 12:31; 14:30; 2 Cor. 4:4; Eph. 2:2; 1 John 5:19). He means to recapture that territory for his own glory. So he builds his church as an expression of the presence of his kingdom. Its life operates along the lines of his will and purpose. Christians therefore, no matter what their earthly citizenship is, belong first and foremost to the city that Jesus Christ is building; their ultimate 'citizenship is in heaven' (Phil. 3:20).

These words had a special meaning for the first members of the little church in Philippi. It was a Roman colony. As excavations of old Roman towns outside Italy make clear, the Romans built cities the way supermarkets, retail or fast-food chain stores tend to be built—walk into one store or fast-food restaurant and you immediately recognize the brand. There is a company blueprint on which it has been modelled. There is a 'brand' style. So in a Roman colony the pattern of the streets, the theatre, and the baths would all be recognizably laid out according to the 'Roman' pattern. However different the locations might be, and the scenery beyond, and however varied the details of houses and other buildings, the basic pattern was instantaneously recognizable.

The same is true of the church. Churches differ in geographical location, ethnic make-up, language, educational opportunities, social standing and much more. But each congregation (as well as the church as a whole) is an outpost of heaven. The worship, the basic structure of fellowship, the spiritual atmosphere of any church should remind us of every other true church—we should be able to taste heaven on earth in every congregation.

This leads us to an important question. If we were to ask: 'So what "qualifies" me to be a member of this church?' the basic answer is: 'The same as "qualifies" you for entrance into heaven!'

Of course the 'qualification' is not a certain standard of life or spirituality we have attained. It is a recognition that we can never attain God's standard, and that we are accepted by him only through faith in Christ. And it is also true that we can never assess perfectly the heart of another human being, or even our own. But since citizenship in the church on earth reflects citizenship in heaven, the 'entry requirement' must be one and the same: our confession of a living faith in Jesus Christ as Saviour and Lord. If I cannot make that confession then by all means I should attend church. I should pay close attention to others who are members, to see if I can work out from the teaching I hear and from the people I meet, what a real Christian is. But I can only *belong* to the church on earth if I have faith in Christ.

It is interesting, in this context, to reflect on what happens in Christian churches. To some what has been said already in this chapter may seem rather rigorous. We have almost assumed the church *needs* members and that churches should or will simply be glad to welcome people as members on their own terms. But if this all seems a little radical, perhaps more demanding than people feel comfortable accepting, it is worth paying attention to something contemporary sociologists have recognized. Research indicates that, typically, churches that adopt any other 'membership' position—and dilute the demanding nature of Christian discipleship—shrink rather than grow.[1] It is churches that echo the New Testament that grow. These are the cities that last.

'City' is a metaphor for the church. But the second picture of the nature of the church that underlies Matthew 16:18 is not a metaphor. It is the reality itself.

The family of God

The English word 'church' translates the Greek word *ekklēsia*. It is a compound noun which means 'the called-out-together.' In the Greek translation of the Old Testament commonly used in the first century AD, it translates the Hebrew word *qahal*, the congregation of the Lord. This language became prominent at the time of the Exodus when the Lord called his people *out of* Egypt and summoned them *together* to worship and serve him as his family. Later he would tell them, 'you alone of the families of the earth I have known' (Amos 3:2), and 'Out of Egypt I have called my son' (Hos. 11:1).

This is the most basic picture of the church in the New Testament. It consists of those who have been given new life by the Spirit's work, and gathered together by faith in Jesus Christ. In fact, as we have suggested, it is not really a picture, an 'image' or a 'metaphor.' Family is what the church *is*.

A moment's thought about the teaching of Jesus should make clear why this is the case. Prominent in his teaching and at the heart of the blessings he gives us is the privilege of calling God 'our Father in heaven.' As J. I. Packer wisely noted:

> If you want to judge how well a person understands Christianity, find out how much he makes of the thought of being God's child,

---

[1] Roger Finke and Rodney Stark, *The Churching of America 1762–2005* (Brunswick, NJ: Rutgers University Press, rev. ed. 2005).

and having God as his Father. If this is not the thought that prompts and controls his worship and prayers and his whole outlook on life, it means that he does not understand Christianity very well.[1]

It follows that through faith in Christ we become members of his family. Together we are able to pray '*Our* Father which art in heaven, hallowed be thy name …'

In human families we often see strong resemblances—the 'family likeness.' Often when standing at the church door at the end of a service, especially at holiday seasons (Christmas, Easter, Thanksgiving in the USA) members have introduced me to family who have travelled to be with them. They may be parents, or siblings, adult children who have flown the nest, or grandchildren. It is fascinating so often to see features of the family likeness reproduced down through the generations. They are often obvious—and the more we look for them the more we see them.

The same is true in the family of God, the church, not only locally but world-wide. I think of an occasion when I spent three days with a small group of Christians from all the continents and a dozen and more different countries. What a wonderful experience to see the same spiritual family traits expressed in people who had not met each other before, and from such different ethnic backgrounds—brothers and sisters in the one family of Jesus Christ. This is the church. And every true Christian experiences this again and again.

But in addition to this, each 'branch' of this family—members of individual congregations—develops particular family traits, as Christ blesses us without homogenizing our ethnic traits, social contexts, and individual personalities. This is why Paul is able to speak about 'the multi-coloured' wisdom of God being put on display 'in the church' (Eph. 3:10).[2]

---

[1] James I. Packer, *Knowing God* (London: Hodder & Stoughton, 1973), p. 182.

[2] The word translated 'varied' is *polupoikilos* and can mean 'multi-coloured' as

There are conclusions that follow from this as we think about becoming a member of a particular church.

Conclusions

Of primary importance, just as it should be true in our natural family so in our local church, we need to feel that there is no other church family to which we would rather belong—even if our congregation is far from perfect.

Yes, there may be bigger churches or (if small is your preference), even smaller ones. Other churches may have better preachers and pastors; there may be more suitable meeting places; there may be contexts that seem more favourable for service and witness. But so long as the Lord has placed you in the particular family branch to which you belong—it should be your desire to be able to say, 'There is no other church in the world I would rather be part of just now!'

I remember standing with an elder of a mega-church I was visiting as new members were being introduced and received. The large number of them stretched far across the room. He leaned over to me and said 'Don't you think this is the greatest church in the world?'

I was glad he thought that. At the same time, I thought, 'Personally, I'd rather be a member of the church I am in! But I am so encouraged that you think like this. I wouldn't have it any other way!' Don't you think we were both right?

If by any chance you are thinking of becoming a member of a local church and you do not even want to be able to say that, perhaps you should refrain from joining it. Indeed, perhaps you should think seriously about whether you are prepared for membership in any church—including the one you think is 'the greatest'!

Why say that? Because one of the things God means to do in and for you in a local church is to work in your life and shape it through

---

it does in the Septuagint (Greek) translation of Gen. 37:3. This is the reason some translations refer to the 'many-colours' of the coat Jacob gave to Joseph.

that particular branch of his family. He has things for you to learn there. Given the unique collection of family members who surround us, the influences of the specific preaching we hear, and the unique sphere in which each church family is set—there is inevitably something distinctive and wonderfully unique about Christians in each congregation. God is not in the business of producing clones. He loves to see variety as well as similarity!

A friend once told me of an experience he had. At an international gathering of distinguished lawyers he had walked down a stairway into the reception area. Someone approached him and asked: 'Do you, by any chance, belong to _____ Church?' Somewhat astonished my friend confirmed that indeed he did! The stranger was exactly right. How did he know? There must have been something about my friend that triggered off a connection in his mind to that particular branch of the family of God.

The influence on our lives of belonging to the church, to the family of Christ, goes that deep. That is why a true Christian learns to love the church. It is Christ's love, the apple of his eye, the passion of his heart.

If Jesus Christ is your Saviour, and if he loved the church and died for the church (Eph. 5:25), are you prepared to live in and for that church for which he died? That is a core value. And it is church membership in a nutshell.

Appendix

The following example of Rotary Club membership rules is downloaded, virtually at random, from the web page of the Trenton Branch (New Jersey, USA):

1. Why make such a big deal out of meeting attendance?

The attendance rules may at times seem unnecessarily rigid, but being present at club meetings is one of the basic obligations a member accepts on joining a Rotary club. The constitutional rules emphasize that Rotary is a participatory organization that highly values regular attendance. When a member is absent the entire club loses the personal association with that member, and the member loses touch with the activities of the club. Attendance is the 'glue' that holds the club together and provides the basic framework for service. It is a vital part of the operation and success of every Rotary club.

2. What are the basic Rotary rules for meeting attendance?

Except for members specifically granted an attendance exemption by the Board of Directors (see below), all Active members are expected to:

• Attend or make up at least 50% of club regular meetings in each half of the year.

• Attend at least 25% of this club's regular meetings in each half of the year.

• If a member fails to attend as required in (a) and (b) above, the member's membership shall be subject to termination unless the Board consents to such non-attendance for good cause.

• Unless excused by the Board for good and sufficient reason, each member who fails to attend or make up four consecutive regular meetings shall be informed by the Board that the member's non-attendance may be considered a request to terminate membership in this club. Thereafter, the Board, by a majority vote, may terminate the member's membership.

3. What happens if I miss a weekly meeting?

As you can see from the above, Rotary rules strongly encourage you to make up for missed meetings of this club by attending another club's weekly meeting. You will be given credit for a makeup if, within 14 days before or after the missed meeting, you:

• Attend a regular meeting of another Rotary club, including their debunking; or

• Attend a Trenton Rotary Club event held in lieu of a regular meeting; or

• Attend a regular meeting of a Rotaract or Interact club; or D. Attend a Board meeting of Trenton Rotary Club, Trenton Rotary Foundation, or

• Attend a convention, meeting or fellowship activity of R.I. and certain other international events, a Rotary district conference, a Rotary district assembly, a Rotary district training/workshop, any district committee meeting held by direction of the District Governor.

4. Where can I make up a meeting?

You can make up at another Rotary Club meeting anywhere in the world. To find a meeting: Trenton Rotary lists local make-up locations here Rotary International http://www.rotary.org/support/clubs/index.html. You can now make up online by attending an 'e' meeting: http://www.rotary.org/membership/education/makeups.html. When visiting other clubs, obtain a makeup card when you check in, fill it out, and return it to the Club Secretary. PLEASE NOTE: Credit for make-ups is not automatic. In all cases, to receive credit, you must inform the Club Secretary by submitting a makeup card, or email message, or some form of written notification, stating the club or event attended and the date, and the date of the missed meeting for which you want the makeup to apply.

5. Are there provisions in the rules for excused absences or attendance exemptions?

Yes. A member's absence may be excused if:

A. the absence complies with the conditions and under circumstances approved by the Board. The Board may excuse a member's absence for reasons which it considers to be good and sufficient; or

B. the member is eligible for an attendance exemption under the so-called Rule of 85. For this to apply, the aggregate of the member's years of age and years of membership in one or more Rotary clubs is 85 years or more, and the member has submitted a written request to the Board, and the Board has approved the request.

6. Can I get credit for attending a meeting or a makeup if I have to leave the meeting early?

Yes. A member can be counted as attending either a regular or makeup meeting if he or she is present for at least 60% of the meeting, or is present and is called away unexpectedly and subsequently produces evidence to the satisfaction of the Board that such action was reasonable.

7. Can I be excused for missing a meeting if I am ill?

Yes, but only for a protracted illness. Remember, you have two weeks after a missed meeting to attend another club's meeting to make up. So, to be excused due to illness, the illness must extend for at least a week or 10 days. If you are ill for a longer period of time, it is possible for the Board to grant an excused absence. See 5(a) above.

8. If I am traveling out of the country, are there special attendance rules that apply?

Yes, in certain circumstances, although they are not too common. If you are planning an extended trip abroad, and think you may have problems making up, you may want to see the Club Secretary for any special attendance rules that may apply.

9. If I am on jury duty and am unable to attend a regular club meeting, do I have to make up?

Yes. There is no provision for granting attendance credit to a member who is absent from a club meeting because of jury duty.

10. Who do I pay for the make-up meeting?

Pay the club that you visit for the meal.[1]

---

[1] Downloaded from http://www.trentonrotary.org/attendance_rules.php, 12 September 2016.

2

What Is Your Story?

or

Are You a Christian?

A living church is very different from what most outsiders imagine it to be. It is not primarily an organization (although it should not be disorganized!). Nor is it merely a building (although it may have several). It is a family.

You mean 'It is *like* a family'? No. We rightly say the church is *like* a flock of sheep. But the church is not simply 'like' a family. It *is* a family—God's family. He is our Father; we are his children; we have become brothers and sisters. Indeed, as we have seen, there is a profound sense in which the church is a more basic family than even our own natural family.

So, the next question on our minds should be: How, then, do I become a member of this family, the church?

Churches have their own process to welcome people as 'members.' Some churches ask prospective members to come for an interview with one or two of the leaders. Others organize a series of group meetings, a 'New Members' Class' or an 'Inquirers' Class' designed to help those who have been coming around the church for a while and are thinking about the next stage of becoming 'members' in a formal way. These are sometimes also an opportunity for people who know little or nothing about the Christian faith to find out more about the Christian gospel and discover what church life is like. Then probably they will meet with a couple of the church leaders in a relatively informal setting to talk things though. If they become members then they will usually be welcomed publicly at a church service, when they will be asked to respond to a short series of commitment questions.

Imagine, if you will, the following scene. Groups of church leaders are meeting with three couples to discuss church membership with them. We can call them 'Mr and Mrs Faithful,' 'Mr and Mrs Natural,' and 'Mr and Mrs Joiner.'[1] Let's imagine their conversations.

The Faithfuls

After some friendly conversation one of the leaders says:

'Mr and Mrs Faithful, we're glad you have been coming to our New Members' Class. We hope you have enjoyed them. People often tell us they have found them a helpful preparation for membership. Now, you have been coming around the church long enough to know that when we welcome new friends we always have that series of questions we ask them at the welcome service. So in our meeting today we simply want to get to know you both a little more and to ask you to tell us about how you both came to faith in Christ.'

'Of course,' reply both of the Faithfuls at the same time. 'You go first, Jim.' And so they each tell their story. Mr Faithful came from a non-Christian home and became a Christian through some fellow students when he went to university. Mrs Faithful was brought up in a Christian home and says that although she has had some growth spurts and the occasional crisis in her faith she cannot remember any specific moment when she came to faith; her experience has been more like a seed growing into a flower, she says.

---

[1] With apologies to John Bunyan's *The Pilgrim's Progress* for the rather obvious-sounding names!

'So,' says Jim Faithful, 'our pathways have been a little different, but we know we both trust in Christ as our Saviour and Lord!'

The Naturals

In the next room, Mr and Mrs Natural are sitting in similar chairs, with two other leaders. The conversation begins in much the same way, but one of the leaders here is a little more direct in his first question:

'Mr and Mrs Natural, would you say that you are already Christian believers?'

'Well,' says Mr Natural, very quickly, 'Of course we are—naturally [if you will forgive the pun]—we've been members of churches wherever we have lived, and we actually met in a church youth group. Yes, I'd say we are Christians. We have been all our lives.'

The other elder smiles gently, and says 'You really are "Church people" Mr Natural! But tell us a little more about your faith in the Lord Jesus. Incidentally,' he adds, 'I am interested to know—were you ever asked that question when you became a member of those other churches?'

'Well, no,' says Mrs Natural. 'No one has ever asked us such a question! They've known we have been church people all our lives. What do you mean by asking us if we are Christians? Nobody has ever asked me that question!'

'Well, then,' says the elder, very gently—'that's interesting. How do you both think about what it means to be a Christian?'

'Well, I suppose it all depends on what you mean,' Fred Natural replies; 'it is very personal isn't it? I have always tried to be a Christian. I do my best. I think I am … I don't mean I am perfect … but I think I'm probably at least as good as most. …' Noting his hesitation, Mrs Natural interjects: 'Fred, of course you have *always* been a Christian; you are one of the nicest people anyone could know!'

The Joiners

The interview with Mr and Mrs Joiner begins in a third room in a similar way. It turns out that Mr Joiner is actually not a joiner but an accountant. The same question comes:

'Mr Joiner, how did you become a Christian?' But before he can answer Mrs Joiner says (perhaps a little too quickly?): 'Now, we *are church members*. All we want to do is to *transfer our membership*. We have done this before—although we have never had to go to a class for two months, to be quite honest. We just want to transfer our membership, that's all.'

'Indeed,' says the other elder, patiently (this is not the first time he has met a Mrs Joiner!). 'But, you know, the great thing—and, to be honest, the really important thing—is our faith in Christ, isn't it, and our desire to live for him?'

'But we have NEVER been asked such a question when we have joined churches in the past,' says Mary Joiner.

'Well, Mrs Joiner,' responds the other elder again, very sweetly, 'That's really quite interesting, isn't it? Maybe that's one of the Lord's reasons for leading us to ask it this morning. What would you say if someone else—I don't mean us here this morning—perhaps one of your friends or colleagues said to you "Mary, what is a Christian? Do you know? Are *you* a Christian, Mary? If you are, would you tell me your story? For some reason, I think I would like to find out more about this Christianity business." How would you go about it? Would you tell her your own story—we'd love to hear it.'

We can leave the Joiners now with those questions—'Are *you* a Christian? ... Would you tell me your story?'—still unanswered, hanging in the air.

Being a Christian

So, what is a Christian? And why should a Christian have a 'story'?

The question 'What is your story?' is a great way to strike up a conversation with a stranger who comes to sit beside you in church—(or for that matter anywhere!). People usually appreciate the fact that you are interested in knowing about them. They may even be relieved that you are not one of those people who are always talking about themselves!

I could tell you my story. But a better idea would be to call in a really expert witness—someone whose story has helped countless others to become Christians—all across the socio-economic, moral, and ethnic ranges.

I mean Saul of Tarsus.

Saul (or Paul—we tend to know him by his Roman name[1]) tells his story, or parts of it, several times over in the New Testament narrative. It is told three times in the Acts of the Apostles. In his letters he describes it from several different angles. Taken together they make for fascinating reading.

In Acts the story is told 'from the outside'—saying essentially 'Here is what happened.' But in his letters Paul tells it 'from the inside.' One of those places—perhaps the most fascinating—is in Philippians chapter 3. Here, writing to perhaps his favourite church (he calls them his 'joy and crown' in Phil. 4:1), he explains what happened:

> Finally, my brothers, rejoice in the Lord. To write the same things to you is no trouble to me and is safe for you. Look out for the dogs, look out for the evildoers, look out for those who mutilate the flesh. For we are the real circumcision, who worship by the Spirit of God and glory in Christ Jesus and put no confidence in the flesh—though I myself have reason for confidence in the flesh also. If anyone else thinks he has reason for confidence in the flesh, I have more: circumcised on the eighth day, of the people of Israel, of the

[1] Paul was both a Jew and a Roman citizen and presumably functioned in one world using his Jewish name and in the other using his Roman name—perhaps a little like friends (I have at least two) who are known by one name in their family and friends and another in their business life.

tribe of Benjamin, a Hebrew of Hebrews; as to the law, a Pharisee; as to zeal, a persecutor of the church; as to righteousness, under the law blameless. But whatever gain I had, I counted as loss for the sake of Christ. Indeed, I count everything as loss because of the surpassing worth of knowing Christ Jesus my Lord. For his sake I have suffered the loss of all things and count them as rubbish, in order that I may gain Christ and be found in him, not having a righteousness of my own that comes from the law, but that which comes through faith in Christ, the righteousness from God that depends on faith— that I may know him and the power of his resurrection, and may share his sufferings, becoming like him in his death, that by any means possible I may attain the resurrection from the dead (Phil. 3:1-11).

Of course Paul's experience was very dramatic. After all, he had the original 'Damascus Road Experience'! But here he is describing the inside story rather than the external drama.

The 'outside story' Christians have will be as varied as they themselves are. But 'the inside stories' tend to share important characteristics.

The story unfolds in three stages.

Stage number 1: Paul by nature

In earlier life Paul went by the Jewish name of 'Saul' rather than his Roman name 'Paul.' He may have received both names as a child since he was brought up as a Jew in Tarsus, an international city in the Roman Empire. From the beginning two cultures met, perhaps even collided, in his life. He was brought up as an orthodox Jew who was at the same time born a Roman citizen. When he became a missionary-apostle to Gentiles it was natural enough that he would use his 'Gentile' name, and that is how he has been known ever since.

Saul was a very orthodox Jew. By both natural heredity and personal choice his credentials were impeccable:

I myself have reason for confidence in the flesh also. If anyone else thinks he has reason for confidence in the flesh, I have more:

By heredity:

- circumcised on the eighth day,
- of the people of Israel,
- of the tribe of Benjamin,
- a Hebrew of Hebrews;

By personal choice:

- as to the law, a Pharisee;
- as to zeal, a persecutor of the church;
- as to righteousness, under the law blameless.

When it came to reasons for confidence in what he was by nature, he had them all. He could trace his family tree back to the Patriarchs and specifically to the tribe which had given Israel her first king (after whom he was probably named). His parents were Hebrew speakers and had brought him up as a bi- and probably tri-lingual child—but Hebrew was his native tongue. He had personally chosen to belong to the strictest of the Jewish sects, the Pharisees. As far as the law was concerned he regarded himself as 'blameless.' He may not have been perfect (where have we heard that before?), but no one could point an accusatory finger at him. He was not only 'as good, if not better than most,' he had made it a point to be actually better than everyone else. His claim that 'I was advancing in Judaism beyond many of my own age' (Gal. 1:14) is probably simply a polite way of saying it was his ambition to be *numero uno*.

Paul never denied that he was the recipient of tremendous privileges. In Romans 9:4 he lists even more in which he shared: 'adoption, the glory, the covenants, the giving of the law, the worship, and the promises.' Yet, God needed to bring him, by a very hard road, to see that he had actually missed the whole point of these blessings. It was not that he later came to despise them. In themselves they were remarkable advantages. But they were intended to be signposts on the road, not the destination of the journey. And, sadly, Saul had been looking at the signposts instead of seeing where they pointed. They were all meant to point him to Jesus. But he so misread them that he was actually resisting Jesus. More than that, he had started to persecute anyone who believed in Jesus. His is a unique story from one point of view (the greatest persecutor of the church becomes its greatest theologian and evangelist). His story was certainly more dramatic than most. But his spiritual condition was common enough among his own people—many of whom, like Saul, were familiar with the signposts, but failed to see where they were pointing. It was as though there was a veil over their hearts (2 Cor. 3:15).

A similar story has been repeated again and again in the Christian era—when having Christian parents, and a Bible, and the signs of baptism and the Lord's Supper, or strict religious priorities, have been substituted and misread for a right relationship with God. It was this that Saul eventually realized he lacked, that he needed, and that by God's grace he later received.

Like many others, my own story is a much less dramatic version of the same reality. Although I was not brought up in a church-going home, I began to read the Bible when I was about nine. For five years I read it, systematically, every day. If someone had asked me 'Are you a Christian?' I probably would have said, 'Well, I hope so: I read the Bible, I pray, and I do what I can to help others.'

Then, one memorable day, as I was reading John's Gospel, some words of Jesus seemed to walk off the page and right into my life:

> You search the Scriptures because you think that in them you have eternal life; and it is they that bear witness about me, yet you refuse to come to me that you may have life (John 5:39-40).

I think it might be more accurate to say that Jesus himself seemed to walk out of the book and show me myself in a totally new light. I had already amassed a substantial knowledge of the contents of the Bible. I realize now that this providence was a great privilege, and I am grateful for it. But I had missed the whole point of the Bible's message. I had read it as though it was encouraging me basically to do my best, to try to follow the example of Jesus. I had been blind to the fact that it was a signpost to Jesus himself. In all the good things I was trying to do I had not come to realize my need of a Saviour. Now the truth became clear: I too had never come to him that I might have life!

I suspect that is a not uncommon story.

Stage number 2: Paul discovers the truth about himself

But perhaps the most intriguing thing Paul says (which I would never have dreamed of saying!) is that as far as he could tell, he was 'under the law blameless.' He says something similar later when he speaks about 'having my own righteousness according to the law' (Phil. 3:9).

There is a kind of religion just like that, isn't there, that many people confuse with being a Christian.

Over the years some words, permanently associated with the voice of Frank Sinatra, have been a popular choice for music at the end of funerals in the United Kingdom:

> To think I did all that,
> And may I say,
> Not in a shy way;
> Oh no, oh no, not me—
> I did it my way.[1]

---

[1] 'My Way' was recorded by Frank Sinatra in late December 1968 and released in 1969. Written by the singer-song writer Paul Anka it was based on a French original.

People still often say, 'Heaven helps those who help themselves.' There is a religious form of the same words. It is well illustrated in Jesus' parable of 'The Tax Collector and the Pharisee.' He describes the Pharisee's prayer as follows:

> God, *I thank you*
>   that *I* am not like other men
>   or even like this tax collector ...
>   that *I* fast twice a week
>   that *I* give tithes of all that *I* get (Luke 18:11-12).

Isn't it telling that in these words the Pharisee says 'you' (i.e. God) only once but 'I' five times?

Something very profound happened to Saul of Tarsus that changed all this. He does not explain here in great detail how it happened; but he does tell us that he came to see that his confidence in 'a righteousness of my own' was badly misplaced. Somehow the law of God got inside his skin and he came to realize that he was a sinner who needed a Saviour, not a righteous man at all. And all the time the Lord was working in his life to bring him to the point where he would recognize Christ Jesus was the Saviour he needed. And so, halted in his tracks and blinded on the Damascus Road, and taken to Straight Street where he was visited by Ananias, he was baptized as a new believer in Jesus Christ. One can only imagine the tremendous shock it must have been to him not only to be met by Jesus, but to discover that he had been so badly wrong, to realize that his own righteousness was paper thin—to be brought to see that he was a sinner.

Of course, our story may have different twists and turns. A disappointment or failure may cause us to think about where our life is heading. Someone's death can do it, or equally a baby's birth. Or perhaps there is something we notice in a friend or colleague, and we cannot quite put our finger on the explanation—except that they are known as a Christian. And it makes us think, 'There is something about him I don't understand,' or 'She seems to know something I don't; she certainly has something I lack.' We may be irritated by the fact that their lives silently condemn ours. I remember hearing a remarkable story about several top class professional golfers who had played a round of golf with Dr Billy Graham. After the game one of them was complaining in the locker room about Dr Graham 'going on and on about Christ through the whole round.' One of the other golfers turned to him and said 'But Billy Graham didn't even mention his name!'

The night I became a Christian I listened to the story of a young business man. His story went something like this. In his workplace he regularly passed the door of the company 'typing pool.' That expression itself dates me, and perhaps requires explanation! It was the office in which secretaries typed (yes, on typewriters!) letters or other documents which their bosses had earlier dictated to them.

One day as the young man passed the typing pool he said to a colleague, 'Every time I pass that door there always seems to be one of those typists working away with a regularity that the others don't have!' The enigma had obviously begun to play on his mind a little. His colleague's casually-spoken response was, if anything, even more enigmatic. 'Oh,' he said, 'that will be _____. *She's a Christian'*—leaving the young man to wonder what the connection between typing and Christianity might be! The enigma was like bait on a hook; he had swallowed it; he could not struggle free. It led eventually to him becoming a Christian. As it happened, having heard this story so did I. I have often wondered if somehow I would ever meet the girl in the typing pool, to thank her. Not yet; but one day.

When he wrote his letter to the Philippians Paul knew that, sitting listening to it being read out to the church, and hearing the inside story of his coming to faith, would be three people he knew well. One had become a Christian partly by being caught in an earthquake, another had been enslaved to and abused by wicked men who had groomed her for their own vile purposes. Her behaviour had prompted Paul to exorcize evil spirits from her in Jesus' name and set her free. These two had dramatic conversion stories. But the third person (who was the first to come to faith) was quite different, and her story totally undramatic. She had been sitting quietly in a group of praying women, listening to Paul speak about Jesus, when her heart was opened.[1] All three were Christians, but each one was brought to Christ by a different path.

These different circumstances and paths that bring us eventually to faith are of God's choosing and making. But what they have in common is the result: we come to trust in the Lord Jesus as our Saviour and to follow him as our Lord. Discovering that we have neither righteousness of our own nor resources to acquire it either slowly or suddenly reveals our need of Christ, the message of the gospel penetrates hearts that the Holy Spirit has been softening, and we yield. Thus it was for Saul of Tarsus. Thus it is for us too.

Stage number 3: What Paul discovered by grace

Of course, all this was only the beginning. Paul goes on to tell us that there was much more to discover about Christ *after* he became a Christian. He had tried to build his own right standing before God on the basis of the law. Now he realized that Jesus had lived a life of perfect obedience in his place. More, Jesus had become obedient specifically 'to the death of the cross'—that is, he had come under God's judgement curse for our sins (Phil. 2:8; Gal. 3:13). By his death he cancelled out Paul's debt; and by his life of obedience on Paul's behalf, Jesus had woven the 'righteousness from God' which he had now received 'through faith in Christ.' This was righteousness from God, received through faith, and given in Christ (Phil. 3:9).

All his life Saul had attempted to create his own righteousness. He now learned what Jesus had spoken about in his Sermon on the

---

[1] See Acts 16:11-34 for the stories.

Mount: 'Unless your righteousness exceeds that of the scribes and Pharisees, you will never enter the kingdom of heaven' (Matt. 5:20). This, as he at last discovered, is the righteousness that God provides in Christ for those who trust in him.

The result? It took Paul all his thirteen New Testament letters to explain what it means to come to faith in Christ. But it included this sevenfold blessing:

- Union and communion with Jesus Christ

- The forgiveness of his sins

- Relief from a sense of guilt and shame for his past failures

- Deliverance from the reign of sin and the powers of darkness over his life

- Being brought into the family of God and being able to call him 'Abba,' Father

- The assured hope of eternal life

- A new desire to become like Jesus—even if it meant hardship in this world

Thus he wrote about his new desire—

> … that I may know him and the power of his resurrection, and may share his sufferings, becoming like him in his death … I press on toward the goal for the prize of the upward call of God in Christ Jesus … who will transform our lowly body to be like his glorious body, by the power that enables him even to subject all things to himself. (Phil. 3:10, 14, 21)

If this is the destiny of Christians, why would anyone not want to become one?

Which way?

When it comes to being a Christian, 'my way' does not work.

One of the saddest things in the world is to see people who are connected to the church yet disconnected from Jesus. All the signposts are in place around them; but they have never seen where they are pointing—to him. They speak of living by the Sermon on the Mount, but forget how that sermon ends with Jesus saying:

> Not everyone who says to me, 'Lord, Lord,' will enter the kingdom of heaven, but the one who does the will of my Father who is in heaven. On that day many will say to me, 'Lord, Lord, did we not prophesy in your name, and cast out demons in your name, and do many mighty works in your name?' And then will I declare to them, 'I never knew you; depart from me, you workers of lawlessness.' (Matt. 7:20-23)

It is apparently possible:

- to do *works* and yet not be a Christian

- to do *many* works and yet not be a Christian

- to do many *mighty* works and yet not be a Christian

- to do many mighty works *in Jesus' name* and yet not be a Christian

- to *call Jesus 'Lord'* and yet not be a Christian

How can this be?

Because becoming a Christian is not the result of our works but of the Lord Jesus' works! We become Christians by faith, not by works. Otherwise we hear Jesus' words but fail to do them. Rather than being people who build our spiritual house on a rock, we build it on sand, and it collapses. This is the very point Jesus made as he brought the Sermon on the Mount to a conclusion.

I heard of a little boy who used to help his mum whenever she took part in the church-cleaning day. The congregation knew that as he moved around the building with his little duster, helping her clean, he would sing his favourite Bible song:

The wise man built his house upon the rock
The wise man built his house upon the rock
The wise man built his house upon the rock
And the rain came tumbling down

Oh, the rain came down
And the floods came up
The rain came down
And the floods came up
The rain came down
And the floods came up
And the house on the rock stood firm.

The foolish man built his house upon the sand
The foolish man built his house upon the sand
The foolish man built his house upon the sand
And the rain came tumbling down

Oh, the rain came down
And the floods came up
The rain came down
And the floods came up
The rain came down
And the floods came up
And the house on the sand fell flat.

So, build your house on the Lord Jesus Christ …

Some time later, the little boy became gravely ill and died. At the end of his funeral service, as his casket was carried from the church, the organist began to play a familiar piece of music:

The wise man built his house upon the rock …

I think about that little boy, whom I never knew, quite often. Through his short life the Lord was teaching everyone who knew him a wonderful lesson. Understanding the gospel and becoming a Christian is not a matter of age, or intellect. It is a matter of being helped to realize that you have no righteousness of your own and that you need Christ, coming to trust him by God's grace, turning away from the sin that has so mastered your life, and building your life on him. A child can understand and do that. And yet, sadly, many intelligent adults never do. They assume that at the end of the day being a Christian is about trying to get a pass mark. But that is the sure way to fail. We can never find acceptance with a holy God on the basis of what we have done. Like Saul of Tarsus, no matter what our religious pedigree may be, the righteousness we seek to establish is inadequate. We need the righteousness that God provides. And that comes to us only through faith in Christ.

Your story?

So—if someone were to say to you: 'Are you a Christian? I'd love to hear your story'—would you have one to tell?

It could begin in a very dramatic way, like Paul's; or it could be comparatively undramatic, like mine. Either way, at its heart will be this:

- I knew I could not stand before God as I am in my sin and failure

- I learned that Jesus Christ is able to save anyone who comes to him

- I turned to and trusted in Christ—and now I am clothed in his righteousness

- Now I want to know him, love him more, and serve him

So we end this chapter where we began, with the question, 'Are you a Christian?' Is there something in your heart that responds, 'Yes! Yes! I am'? If not, put this book down, think about the question, and ask the Lord to help you to see why you need a Saviour, and why it is that Jesus Christ is the Saviour you need.

3

Follow My Leader

or

Being a Disciple

I t is not possible to be a Christian unless you are a disciple of the Lord Jesus Christ. In fact, in the earliest days of the Christian church, the term 'disciple' was used of Jesus' followers much more frequently than 'Christian' (Acts 11:26).[1]

The English word 'disciple' is derived from the Latin word *discipulus* which in turn comes from the verb *discere,* to learn, get to know, become familiar with. A disciple is a learner, but not just in the sense of 'someone who goes to school to learn from books.' Perhaps the word 'apprentice' better captures the idea. For a disciple attaches himself or herself to a master in order to learn, to imitate, and to understand. Think of the great European artists and you will get the idea. Art historians speak of a painting being done by someone (perhaps unknown) from 'The School of' a great artist whose name and work we know well. The unknown artist attached himself to the master, learned how to paint from him, used his style, imitated his work, and thus became his *disciple.*

When we become church members we are saying 'I too am a disciple of Jesus. He is not only my Saviour; he is also my Master. I am

---

[1] 'Disciple' or 'disciples' occurs a dozen times in the Acts of the Apostles before the word 'Christian' makes its first appearance.

35

committed to serving him, learning from him, and imitating him so that I can grow to be like him.' In fact, in the New Testament, being a Christian essentially involves becoming more and more like Jesus. This fits in with God's ultimate goal for our lives: 'For those whom he foreknew he also predestined to be conformed to the image of his Son, in order that he might be the firstborn among many brothers' (Rom. 8:29).

This kind of discipleship is not an optional extra to membership. Without it we are only 'paper members'—that is to say, we may be attached to a church, but we do not really belong to Jesus. We are not really members at all!

If this is true (which it is), there is an important question we all need to ask about membership in any church. It is this: 'I realize that a member is a disciple of Jesus. But how does this church understand that? What does the style of discipleship here involve?'

The answer to that question is not something each church makes up for itself. True, churches have different patterns of life together that will shape the answer. But every church should be able to say: 'Our Master has taught us what it means to be a disciple. We use his definition. And then we apply it to life in our fellowship here.'

So, what is Jesus' definition?

Jesus' early followers learned what it meant to be his disciples, first of all, by simply being with him, watching him, and listening to his teaching about the kingdom of God. But as his ministry continued, and especially when he found huge crowds of people coming to watch what he did and to listen to what he taught, he spelled out what it really means to follow him.

Luke's Gospel gives this graphic account of one such occasion:

> Now great crowds accompanied him, and he turned and said to them, If anyone comes to me and does not hate his own father and mother and wife and children and brothers and sisters, yes, and even his own life, *he cannot be my disciple*. Whoever does not bear his own

cross and come after me *cannot be my disciple*. For which of you, desiring to build a tower, does not first sit down and count the cost, whether he has enough to complete it? Otherwise, when he has laid a foundation and is not able to finish, all who see it begin to mock him, saying, 'This man began to build and was not able to finish.' Or what king, going out to encounter another king in war, will not sit down first and deliberate whether he is able with ten thousand to meet him who comes against him with twenty thousand? And if not, while the other is yet a great way off, he sends a delegation and asks for terms of peace. So therefore, any one of you who does not renounce all that he has *cannot be my disciple*.

Salt is good, but if salt has lost its taste, how shall its saltiness be restored? It is of no use either for the soil or for the manure pile. It is thrown away. He who has ears to hear, let him hear. (Luke 14:25-35)

Why does Jesus express himself so negatively (*'cannot be my disciple'*)? In order to make himself clear to the crowd—and in a sense in order to limit the field. Crowds, he knew, can be dangerous for your spiritual well-being. You can be in the crowd, caught up in its enthusiasm, near enough to Jesus in that sense—yet not really think about what is involved in being a disciple.

I had a schoolteacher who used an expression I rarely hear now: 'there can be no *dubiety* about this ...' She meant, of course, 'There can be no debating this, no doubt about its truth, no questioning its reality. This is a fact ...' Jesus is saying that here. There is to be no *dubiety* when it comes to being disciples. Three things mark them:

- They hate father, mother, wife, children, brothers, sisters, and their own life.

- They bear their cross and come after Jesus.

- They renounce all they have.

Do these three things characterize your life?

If not, you cannot be Jesus' disciple.

Cannot be! And if you are not a disciple ... you are not a Christian.

But if you are a Christian, you must also be a disciple.

It is just at this point that Mr and Mrs Joiner (whom we met in Chapter 2 above) would probably say, 'All we wanted to do was to join the church ...' Well, this is Jesus' church. His words suggest three radical questions for church leaders to ask potential members:

1. Do you hate father and mother, brothers and sisters and your own life in order to be a disciple of Jesus?

2. Are you bearing the cross and following Jesus?

3. Have you renounced all you have for him?

Can this really be true? Don't these words make us feel like the hearers of Jesus who asked him 'Then who can be saved?' (Luke 18:26).

What do these words of Jesus really mean?

Consecration—settled priorities

Unless I hate my family, and myself—I cannot be a disciple of Jesus. How can this be?

On the assumption that Jesus' teaching did not blatantly contradict God's word or his own practice, it is fairly obvious that he is using hyperbole here—the figure of speech in which we employ exaggeration for the sake of emphasis. Jesus is shocking us into paying attention. We know this because of the fifth commandment to honour our parents. We know it because Jesus teaches us to love even our enemies. How much more then should we love our own families? It would be foolish to think that Jesus would contradict himself so naively.

What then does he mean?

Sometimes he has been understood this way: 'Jesus simply means we are to love him more than we love our families and ourselves.'

But it is more than that, surely. He means we are to love him *far more* than we love anyone else—so much more that, if the occasion arises the way we value him and give him priority (which is what love does) may lead to us being accused of hating our own family members.

Jesus is telling us to imitate him—to be his disciples. Earlier in his Gospel, Luke describes how Jesus' mother and brothers appeared, wanting to speak to him (probably concerned about what was happening). What was his response when he was told they were outside? 'My mother and my brothers are those who hear the word of God and do it' (Luke 8:19-21). Jesus' priorities were radically different from theirs. He was putting natural relationships in a very distant second position. Did some people go away later that day muttering to each other, 'Did you catch what he said there when his family appeared? Does he hate them?'

Why did Jesus focus on family relationships? Why not speak about money, or possessions? In fact, he comes to those things in due time. But first things first. His concern here is obvious. Family relationships are meant to be the greatest blessings we have. Marriage was given by God as the apex of his gifts to Adam (Gen. 1:27; 2:21-24). Children are more important than life itself to loving parents.

But for that very reason these relationships can be the source of greatest spiritual temptation and become the strongest spiritual hindrances—because it is so easy to put them first, instead of the Lord Jesus.

A husband can easily make it clear by his attitude, and even by his words, that he expects his wife to put him first—not the Lord Jesus. A wife can put her wishes and interests before any concern she has that Jesus should have first place in her husband's life. When children come, love and devotion to Christ can be subordinated to our desire for our children to 'get the best' or to 'succeed.' We lose sight of the fact that since Christ has given us everything loyalty to him is our first priority.

I remember as a young teenage Christian reading a mother's anguished letter in the correspondence page of our local newspaper. Her daughter had received a fine education at high school and university, in a day when perhaps only five per cent of the population had that privilege. The world lay at the daughter's feet. But she had sensed Christ's call on her life and was going overseas to serve as a missionary. Her mother was in despair. Her letter was a *cri de couer*. Could nobody talk sense into her daughter to show her that she was *wasting her life*?

The idea that a life offered in total consecration to the Lord Jesus could never be wasted—that was simply beyond her ability to grasp. Why was her daughter throwing her life away like this? Did her daughter hate her? It felt like that.

A young man and woman are attracted to each other. They would make a fine couple, according to many people. But the young woman (why is it often the young woman?) senses that there is one thing lacking. The young man does not make it clear, either by his words or his lifestyle, that he wants her to love Christ far more than she loves him. The idea of being happy as a distant second to Christ is intolerable. It cannot be otherwise when he does not love Christ more than he loves his girlfriend. He could never say on his wedding night what Temple Gairdner of Cairo was able to write:

> That I may come near to her,
>   draw me nearer to Thee, than to her;
> that I may know her,
>   make me to know Thee, more than her;
> that I may love her with the perfect love
>   of a perfect heart,
> cause me to love Thee more than her,
>   and most of all.[1]

[1] Constance E. Padwick, *Temple Gairdner of Cairo* (London: SPCK, 1929), p. 92.

So, does Jesus have absolute priority in my life—even over those who are closest to me and most loved by me? Indeed, *especially over them*? Then I am his disciple.

Cross carrying

'Whoever does not bear his own cross and come after me cannot be my disciple' (Luke 14:27).

'We all have to bear our crosses, don't we?' Sometimes people use these very words without reflecting on the source of the metaphor. But Jesus is not speaking here about 'life's trials' in general, 'the cross I have to bear.' Nor would the crowds who listened to him ever have imagined that was what he meant. They had seen men bearing the cross. The Master's words must have acted as a catalyst to remind them of what many of them may have seen: a man on his way to the place of execution being publicly humiliated—as Jesus himself would later be—by being made to carry the instrument of his execution.

We would not imagine Jesus was referring to 'life's trials' if he had said: 'If you are going to be my disciple you will need to submit to a lethal injection' or, 'If you are going to be my disciple you will first need to die by hanging.'

Jesus is saying—this time with graphic visual imagery—that a disciple is someone who is prepared to follow him and 'die' to his or her own plans and submit to God's purposes—whatever they are, wherever they make take us, whatever it will cost. As Paul later wrote: Christ died 'that those who live might no longer live for themselves but for him who for their sake died and was raised' (2 Cor. 5:15). As C. S. Lewis once remarked, 'nothing in you that has not died will ever be raised from the dead.'[1]

---

[1] The words come from the closing paragraph of *Mere Christianity* (1952), *The Complete C. S. Lewis Signature Classics* (San Francisco: Harper, 2003), p. 118.

No one has expressed this in modern times more powerfully than the German theologian Dietrich Bonhoeffer who was executed by the Nazis just as World War II was coming to an end.

I still prize a copy of Bonhoeffer's most famous book, *The Cost of Discipleship*. In it is a card dated 9th August, 1965. It was a present from one of my school teachers as I left home for university. Opening it today I find that all those years ago I marked several passages:

> We can only achieve perfect liberty and enjoy fellowship with Jesus when his command, his call to absolute discipleship, is appreciated in its entirety. Only the man who follows the command of Jesus single-mindedly, and unresistingly lets his yoke rest upon him, finds his burden easy, and under its gentle pressure receives the power to persevere in the right way. The command of Jesus is hard, unutterably hard, for those who try to resist it. But for those who willingly submit, the yoke is easy and the burden is light.
>
> The only man who has the right to say he is justified by grace alone is the man who has left all to follow Christ. Such a man knows the call to discipleship is a gift of grace, and that the call is inseparable from the grace. But those who try to use this grace as a dispensation from following Christ are simply deceiving themselves.
>
> Had Levi [Matthew] stayed at his post, Jesus might have been his present help in trouble, but not the Lord of his whole life. In other words Levi would never have learnt to believe.
>
> Only the obedient believe.
>
> Is there some part of your life which you are refusing to surrender at his behest, some sinful passion, maybe, or some animosity, some hope, perhaps your ambition or your reason? If so you must not be surprised that you have not received the Holy Spirit. The cross is laid on every Christian. The first Christ-suffering which every man must experience is the call to abandon the attachments of this world … The cross is not the terrible ending to an otherwise god-fearing and happy life, but it meets us at the beginning of our communion with Christ. When Christ calls a man, he bids him come and die.[1]

[1] Dietrich Bonhoeffer, *The Cost of Discipleship*, trans R. H. Fuller (London: SCM Press, 1959), pp. 31, 43, 53, 55, 57, 79.

Need more be said? This is why Paul wrote:

But far be it from me to boast except in the cross of our Lord Jesus Christ, by which the world has been crucified to me, and I to the world. (Gal. 6:14)

C. S. Lewis has a vivid illustration of what this involves in his book *The Great Divorce*. He imagines a 'bus trip' of passengers who have come from hell to visit heaven. They are pale, insipid figures. In terms of Lewis' thinking they have become what they always were—empty, light—without the weight of glory in their being. Lewis's guide and interpreter is George MacDonald, the Scottish writer whose work had such an impact on Lewis's imaginative powers.

At one point in the narrative, they see an insubstantial, ghost-like figure with a little red lizard on his shoulder. The red lizard is constantly talking, dominating his life. An angelic figure appears and offers to deliver the ghost by killing the creature. As the angel comes close the ghost cries out 'Stop, you're hurting me.' The angel responds: 'I didn't say it wouldn't hurt; I said I would kill it.'

Of course the ghostly figure has a deep fear—kill the lizard and the angel will kill him in the process!

Eventually (after much debate) the angel kills the lizard. The ghost suddenly becomes substantial—*real* we might say—the lizard turns into a great stallion; the new man who has emerged from the ghost mounts the stallion and rides away gloriously, leaving the astonished C. S. Lewis asking his guide: 'Am I right in thinking the lizard turned into a horse?' To which MacDonald replies in his thick Scottish accent: 'Aye. But it was killed first. Ye'll not forget that part of the story ...'[1]

You won't, will you—when you remember that a church member is a disciple, someone who has responded to Christ's call, and

---

[1] C. S. Lewis, *The Great Divorce.* (New York: MacMillan, 1946), p. 104. The use of the illustration is not an endorsement of MacDonald's (or Lewis's) theology.

taken up the cross? For only then, with our priorities settled, and the cross upon our shoulders, are we really free to live for Christ.

The Cost

There is something about the teaching of Jesus that combines deep-seated logic with a profound knowledge of the human heart. That is why he concludes his teaching on discipleship here by saying, in essence: 'Now, first, sit down and think about it.'

He tells two parables, one from the world of farming and the other from the military arena.

The farmer's folly (Luke 14:28-30)

Farmers in Jesus' day built towers, storage buildings—some small, some large. No right-thinking farmer wants to build the foundation and then discover that he has run out of money. No, he asks his builder 'What is the bottom line? What will be the total cost?' Otherwise all he will have is an aborted attempt at a building.

We call that a 'folly'—a building structure that has no purpose, either because it was built simply for decoration and has no other purpose, or because it is a standing monument to the foolishness of an individual who had grandiose ideas but did not think about whether or not he had the resources to accomplish them. The result? Their name is forever associated with their lack of wisdom—kindly people smile quietly while those of a less gracious nature mock them.

In the Western world today perhaps many Christian churches are viewed as 'follies.' So many ecclesiastical buildings are now transformed into bingo halls, furniture warehouses, night clubs and the like. Others look empty all week long and are thinly populated on a Sunday. The kindly disposed smile benignly and say: 'They're not doing any harm, and I suppose if they get something out of it, we should let them be.' The militant atheist simply mocks and despises the folly of it all.

Sadly, the reason for this is often—church members. We have these great Christian confessions, like the Apostles' Creed, which, next to the Lord's Prayer may be the most frequently repeated words in the world. Whenever we say it we confess that we believe in the most monumental and life-transforming truths:

> I believe in God, the Father Almighty,
> Maker of heaven and earth;
> and in Jesus Christ, his only Son, our Lord:
> Who was conceived by the Holy Ghost,
> born of the Virgin Mary;
> suffered under Pontius Pilate,
> was crucified, dead and buried.
> He descended into hell;
> the third day he rose again from the dead;
> He ascended into heaven,
> and is seated at the right hand of God the Father Almighty;
> from thence he shall come to judge the living and the dead.
> I believe in the Holy Ghost,
> the Holy Catholic Church,
> the communion of saints,
> the forgiveness of sins,
> the resurrection of the body,
> and the life everlasting.
> Amen.

But it must seem doubtful to critics that we really believe it. We have domesticated the whole thing into a religion, a series of personal accomplishments or disciplines, an insipid moral code—something far removed from the sense the Creed conveys of the greatness of God and his mighty in-breaking into history and then into our individual lives. The idea that being a Christian means radical discipleship, putting Jesus Christ before and above everything, including ourselves—would that not be seen as 'perhaps going a little too far'?

Should it surprise us—when a church becomes a 'Decency Society' rather than a 'Disciples of Jesus Community'—that no one has become a Christian there for a couple of generations—and the members wonder why the Society is shrinking, and feel a vague sense of disappointment that their children do not come so regularly, and their grandchildren—well they don't come at all. They have such different lifestyles. It's all very sad.

But the truth is that it is all very predictable. When people think they are following him but have never thought about the cost of discipleship, this result is inevitable—at least according to Jesus. For discipleship it isn't. And therefore it cannot be authentic Christianity.

So, sit down, think it through. *Can you afford the cost of discipleship?* Well, can you?

Salvation is free, but it leads to a discipleship that will cost you everything you have.

The king's decision (Luke 14:31-33)

Jesus then tells another parable, this time a military one. When faced with an army of twenty thousand, a king whose army has only half that number will ask: 'Can I win with what I have?' The alternative to winning is, however, not 'the *status quo.*' No, it is negotiating a peace settlement in which he will lose his power, and perhaps become a vassal of the more powerful king, and be his servant for the rest of his days.

Do you see the point this parable is making? There can be no neutrality when it comes to Jesus. Either we sit down, think through the issue of discipleship, and see it through—or we spend the rest of our lives in bondage to—whatever. It could be family, or a comfortable life, or a compromised faith. And while we think (but rarely say), 'Well, at least I am free from Jesus!' we are not free at all. We are in bondage to a power around which we will constantly need to be readjusting our lives.

So here Jesus is still saying: 'Think it through.'

But the question has changed a little. It is now—Can you afford *not* to pay the cost of discipleship? For in the end, compromise will cost you everything.

This point is driven home by Jesus with a metaphor he seems to have used on several occasions. Once salt loses its saltiness you cannot restore it. Then it isn't even useful for manure. It is simply discarded.

But there is something rather unusual about the way Jesus expresses himself here. He says, literally, that the salt becomes 'foolish.' Yes, when salt loses its saltiness it becomes 'tasteless.' But there is more. Remember the 'folly' of the farmer in Jesus' earlier statement. The professing Christian, the church member who isn't really a disciple, is 'tasteless.' He or she is so like the rest of the world that there is no distinctive flavour in their lives. And sadly, there is a kind of pointlessness about all they do in the life of the church, because there is no reality. There is a folly here. Could there be a sadder folly than this—simply being discarded?

The cross and all it implies for our discipleship features in so many of the hymns churches love to sing.

There is the great hymn of Isaac Watts:

> When I survey the wondrous cross,
> On which the Prince of glory died,
> My richest gain I count but loss,
> And pour contempt on all my pride.
>
> Forbid it, Lord, that I should boast
> Save in the death of Christ my God:
> All the vain things that charm me most,
> I sacrifice them to His blood.
>
> See from His head, His hands, His feet,
> Sorrow and love flow mingled down;
> Did e'er such love and sorrow meet,
> Or thorns compose so rich a crown?
>
> His dying crimson, like a robe,
> Spreads o'er His body on the tree:

> Then am I dead to all the globe,
>   And all the globe is dead to me.
>
> Were the whole realm of nature mine,
>   That were an offering far too small;
> Love so amazing, so divine,
>   Demands my soul, my life, my all.

Or the words of Elizabeth Clephane:

> Beneath the cross of Jesus
>   I fain would take my stand,
> The shadow of a mighty rock
>   Within a weary land;
> A home within the wilderness,
>   A rest upon the way,
> From the burning of the noontide heat,
>   And the burden of the day.
>
> Upon that cross of Jesus
>   Mine eye at times can see
> The very dying form of One
>   Who suffered there for me;
> And from my stricken heart, with tears,
>   Two wonders I confess—
> The wonders of His glorious love,
>   And my own worthlessness.
>
> I take, O cross, thy shadow
>   For my abiding-place;
> I ask no other sunshine than
>   The sunshine of His face;
> Content to let the world go by,
>   To know no gain or loss—
> My sinful self my only shame,
>   My glory all—the cross.

The question is: Do you glory in the cross? Have you counted the cost? Are you Christ's cross-bearing disciple?

4

A Glorious Addiction

or

What Is a Member?

I have a wonderful older friend who has sometimes invited me to play with him at the golf club of which he is a member. The golf course is well known and widely admired, and it is (despite the poor quality of my golf!) a treat to play there with him.

Naturally, with the sun on my back, the turf under my feet, and my ball on the fairway I would turn to him and say, 'This is a treat, thank you! It is a great golf course!' I can see my friend's face now. It relaxes into a quiet smile, and he says, 'Yes, it's such a privilege to belong here.' He always says it. He never says more than that.

There is more to his smile than meets the eye. One day, years ago now, someone, quite inadvertently, let slip to me that the initiation fee to that golf club was around $100,000. And that is just to become a member. 'Wow!' I thought, 'that gives new meaning to my friend's words "It's such a privilege"!'

To be fair to him, I now suspect that part of his smile bespeaks the fact that he paid the initiation fee a long time ago when it was a great deal more affordable! Yet his appreciation for the privilege, his evident enjoyment and love of all that it means to him—the way he shares that privilege with those he counts as friends—is really a wonderful thing to experience.

That—magnified again and again—is what the early Christians felt about being 'members' of the church.

'Membership' is an interesting word. The suffix '-ship' usually means something like 'having the position of, being in the state of, belonging to the category of …' 'Sonship' means belonging to the category of son; 'dealership' means being in possession of the right to deal, and so on.

But how did the term 'membership'—possessing the status of being a 'member'—originate?

Paul uses this language when he speaks about the church. The imagery comes from human anatomy—the various parts of the body are its 'members': arms, legs, ears, eyes, mouth, hands, and feet. The parts are very different from each other: they look different and they act differently. Yet there is an organic connection and unity among the parts. Each part needs the other parts for the body to function properly. There is a mutual dependence among the parts. We are not all eyes—but how much more difficult it would be for our hands if we were not able to see. Not to put too fine a point on it, the members of the body are both literally and metaphorically 'stuck' with each other!

The head of this 'body' is Jesus Christ. We are all under his direction and lordship. And when the body is working properly it is the most wonderful thing in the world to belong to the church and to love the church. After all, Christ loved the church and gave himself for her (Eph. 5:25). It is, therefore, normal for those who belong to Christ to love the church and give themselves for her too.

This was exactly what the first Christians felt. They loved the church; and they could hardly wait for opportunities to be together.

In 'Part Two' of his account of the beginnings of Christianity, Luke describes what this was like in the first of several 'State of the Church' reports he provides in the early chapters of Acts:

And they devoted themselves to the apostles' teaching and fellow-ship, to the breaking of bread and the prayers. And awe came upon every soul, and many wonders and signs were being done through the apostles. And all who believed were together and had all things in common. And they were selling their possessions and belongings and distributing the proceeds to all, as any had need. And day by day, attending the temple together and breaking bread in their homes, they received their food with glad and generous hearts, praising God and having favour with all the people. And the Lord added to their number day by day those who were being saved. (Acts 2:42-47)

The first Christians met together every day (Acts 2:46). They were not the last to do so. Later Luke tells us how during Paul's ministry in Ephesus (and therefore presumably elsewhere) the pattern was similar. The Christians in town gathered together on a daily basis to meet with each other and to hear Paul teach them 'the whole counsel of God' (Acts 20:27).[1] Nor was this a flash in the pan—it continued for two years. Did it make an impact? Did it ever! 'All the residents of Asia heard the word of the Lord' (Acts 19:10). That is impact!

The disciples in Jerusalem lived in relatively close proximity to each other and were able to meet frequently for prayer and worship. Their appetite for being taught was such that the apostles were eventually not able to cope with any additional tasks and arranged for assistants to be appointed (Acts 6:1-4).

The pattern of life in the early church was very basic: worship, prayer, fellowship, the teaching of the Scriptures—we hear nothing about programmes or special evangelistic outreach. One cannot help wondering if these basics have become lost in a sea of other activities—sometimes to the point of minimizing, or even excluding what was central to these earliest Christians. Here, in Acts, we

---

[1] The esv footnote to Acts 19:9 reflects an old manuscript tradition which states that Paul hired the lecture hall of Tyrannus from 11 a.m. until 4 p.m. If true, what for the citizens of Ephesus was 'siesta time,' for Christians became 'Scripture time'!

are given a reminder that, whatever else may happen in our church family, we each need to make sure that we keep the main things central and fundamental. The immaturity of the child who prefers the wrapping paper to the gift has its spiritual counterpart—and sometimes woe betide the leader or pastor who attempts to wean us from the wrapping paper!

What then were the hallmarks of membership in the church then—and what does that teach us now?

Luke sums them up in one word: *Devotion*: 'they devoted themselves.'

But devotion has an object. Indeed this devotion has three objects, as we shall see.

Luke employs an interesting verb here. He uses it later in Acts when the God-fearing centurion Cornelius calls 'two of his servants and a devout soldier from among those who *attended* him' (Acts 10:7). You can picture the scene. Military officers often have someone accompanying them who seems glued to their side, whose sole responsibility is to do his commander's every wish. In the same way these early Christians were 'glued to' the church. I have even seen the verb translated, somewhat daringly but quite significantly: 'addicted to,' which perhaps helps us sense how completely absorbing church membership is meant to be. They were addicted to:

1. The apostles' teaching,

2. Their fellow Christians,

3. The worship of God.

This is—if only we could see it—a triple addiction that delivers us from all other addictions; it is, therefore, a blessed addiction indeed!

1. The ministry of the word

The Jerusalem disciples simply could not get enough of the apostles' teaching and preaching. Were they a group of egg-heads? Hardly, since the principal teachers here were Galilean peasants—intelligent men, no doubt, but by the standards of the Jerusalem schools (where bright young men like Saul of Tarsus came to study) they were 'uneducated, common men' (Acts 4:13). But the issue here was not the size of their brains but the burning in their hearts.

The order of books in the New Testament obscures something we would probably have noticed if we were 'Theophilus' for whom Luke wrote both his Gospel and the Acts (Luke 1:3; Acts 1:10). He could easily turn back from reading Acts 2 to the description in Luke 24 of what happened when Jesus taught from the word of God: disciples' hearts burned within them (Luke 24:32). Like John Wesley they felt their hearts 'strangely warmed' as Christ spoke about himself through his word.

The teaching and preaching of the Bible lies at the heart of church life for one reason. It is God's word; it causes hearts to burn; and it transforms lives. This is what we find throughout the New Testament. Here are three examples:

- **John 17:17.** Jesus prays that his disciples will be 'sanctified' through the truth. Simply put, to be 'sanctified' means to be cleaned up and transformed. But what is the truth through which these changes take place? 'Your word is truth,' adds Jesus.

- **Romans 12:1, 2.** Christians are not to be *conformed* to this world but *transformed* by the renewing of our minds. Not—note—by having a high IQ, but in the way the cast of our mind is reshaped by the truth of the gospel as the word of God illumines our understanding, takes hold of our affections, subdues our errant wills, and enables us to live for the glory of God.

- **Colossians 3:16**. We are to let the word of Christ dwell in us richly. What a word-picture this is—Christ's word takes up residence in our life! We become a home in which a guest is welcomed without reservation, given the full run of the house and is free to enjoy everything in it. This is how the disciple responds to the reading and exposition of God's word. He or she says 'Welcome, word of Christ. Go anywhere, explore everywhere, do anything, have everything—the whole house is yours— I am completely at your disposal.'

But how does God's word make this impact? Because of—

- Its *truth*—about God, about our sin and need, about Christ the Saviour—works on our minds, clarifies our confusion, convicts us of failure and sin, and points us to Christ. It persuades us about how things really are in our lives and how Christ is able to transform us.

- Its *grace*—as it points us to Christ—first cleanses, and then stirs up, our affections. We experience what Thomas Chalmers called 'the expulsive power of a new affection.'[1] The way the gospel delivers us from the affections, desires and even addictions of the old life is not by creating a vacuum but by filling us with new desires altogether.

- Its *power*—to overcome the hold of sin in our lives—means that we experience more and more what Charles Wesley famously described: 'He breaks the power of cancelled sin, he sets the prisoner free.'[2]

'Coming to church' is not the same thing as 'belonging'—is it? You can come yet not belong. Apparently it is even possible to 'join' and not belong. Jesus knew that:

---

[1] The title of a famous sermon on 1 John 2:15, preached to his congregation in St John's Church, Glasgow, by Thomas Chalmers (1780–1847), the towering figure in Scottish Presbyterianism in the first half of the nineteenth century.

[2] From the hymn 'O for a thousand tongues to sing' written by Charles Wesley (1707–88).

I am the vine; you are the branches. Whoever abides in me and I in him, he it is that bears much fruit, for apart from me you can do nothing. If anyone does not abide in me he is thrown away like a branch and withers; and the branches are gathered, thrown into the fire, and burned. If you abide in me, and my words abide in you, ask whatever you wish, and it will be done for you. (John 15:5-7)

There is no substitute for devotion to God's word. Anything we do substitute for it never works. The history of the church is littered with the wreckage of such failed attempts.

2. The fellowship of the saints

The apostles' teaching did not take place in a vacuum.

Sometimes the very architecture of our church buildings suggests that being a member is like having a season ticket for a bus commute: you show your ticket, climb on board, face the same way as all the other passengers, are driven to the destination by the man at the front, disembark at the end, and get on with your life.

But becoming a church member is very different from purchasing a season ticket. That is why the expressions 'each other' or 'one another' regularly punctuate the letters the apostles wrote to the young churches. Being a Christian is not an individual thing; it is corporate. We become 'addicted' to each other!

I have always loved church on Sunday nights. There are many reasons for this. Some of them are obvious—there is less rush, more time for 'one another-ing.' During my Christian life I have enjoyed being part of a number of very different churches. But what I have enjoyed most of all has been life in those churches where the building has been full for the evening services, when young and old crowd into the 'sanctuary' and then linger long to talk and to 'one another' (if that were a verb in the English language).

What is this? It is family time. This is our joy. We have expressed our love to our Father for our Saviour. By the Spirit we have sung, prayed, and heard God's voice in his word. We have glorified God and we are enjoying him together. There is nothing like this in all the world.

It was like this in the First Church of Jerusalem. Luke (who had clearly done a great deal of careful research) describes it this way:

> And all who believed were together and had all things in common. And they were selling their possessions and belongings and distributing the proceeds to all, as any had need. (Acts 2:44-45)

The point is not that they were the first communists. Rather, they felt it such a privilege to belong to one another that they treated each other as family. They were so addicted to 'the fellowship' that they shared what they had with anyone who had need.

This was not a primitive kind of communism; there was nothing Marxist about this community—indeed Luke makes it clear that they retained the right of private possession (they had their own homes, for example, Acts 2:46; cf. 5:3, 4). But their addiction to the fellowship made it difficult for a spirit of self-centredness and greed to survive. The little green monsters of pride, self-sufficiency, self-interest, and 'me-firstness,' found themselves starved of oxygen in the atmosphere of grace. That is church. No wonder you can get addicted to church.

These believers were being delivered from their addiction to possessions, to wealth—yes, even to money. Money too? Yes, money too.

In our churches we rarely speak about money—rightly so, perhaps. Leaders may well explain the financial policies of the church to us; sometimes there will be instruction on stewarding our resources, including our finances, wisely and well. The church may have a budget and encourage members to commit to regular giving so that church finances do not become either a burden or a crisis.

The New Testament has virtually nothing concrete to say about our financial contribution to the congregation to which we belong. The teaching Paul gives on 'the collection' was not related to what most churches call 'the offering' or 'the collection.' It refers to a special offering Paul had encouraged the Gentile churches to make for their Jewish fellow-believers (2 Cor. 8–9)—not to financing the life of the congregation, or even foreign missions. Christians believe with Hudson Taylor, the founder of the China Inland Mission (now O[verseas] M[issionary] F[ellowship] International) that 'God's work done in God's way will never lack God's resources.'

But on the other hand the Bible has a great deal to say about how we handle our resources, not least our finances, because so often that is a litmus test of the condition of our hearts. The gospel unglues our wallet from our hand and opens it. But, sadly, the superglue of sin can be difficult to dissolve completely.

In 2008, two sociology professors, Christian Smith and Michael Emerson, in collaboration with Patricia Snell, published a fascinating study of financial stewardship in the churches of North America. It has a very clever title: *Passing the Plate*. Smith and Emerson are not TV hucksters begging, bargaining, or bickering for money. Their book is not a popular tract urging Christians to give more, but a serious academic study based on the gathering and analysis of data by careful research (the book's elite publisher is Oxford University Press). Nevertheless they subtitle the Introduction 'The Riddle of Stingy Giving.' They say that, despite a reputation for generosity:

> American Christians give away relatively little money to religious and other purposes. A sizeable number of Christians give little sums of money. Only a small percent of American Christians give gener-ously, in proportion to what their churches call them to give … most American Christians are remarkably ungenerous.[1]

They go on to note that twenty per cent of professing Christians do not give. They calculate that if only those Christians who are genuinely regular church attenders ('a few times a month or more

[1] Christian Smith, Michael O. Emerson with Patricia Snell, *Passing the Plate*, (New York: Oxford University Press, 2008), p. 3.

frequently') were to give ten per cent of their *after tax income* the result would be that there would be 46 billion dollars (yes billion!) additional (yes, additional!) available to fund ministries of all kinds.

The authors provide several detailed pages of potential ministries that could be funded handsomely (even lavishly) by such giving.[1]

No amount of lecturing, hectoring, pleading, browbeating or begging will accomplish this—at least not for long. Our habits are too ingrained and our addiction to money runs too deep (what Paul calls 'the love of money' literally 'the love of silver,' 1 Tim. 6:10). Only a new and more powerful addiction can transform that.

That is precisely what addiction to the fellowship does.

Someone has well said that the devil teaches us to say about our wealth: 'It is mine, and I am hoarding it.' The world, at its best, teaches us to say, 'It's mine, but I am willing to share some of it.' Only the gospel teaches us to say about our wealth, 'It belongs to Jesus, and for him I will use it.'

Enough said?

There is one further element in this gospel addiction:

3. *The worship of the Lord*

What did these believers do? Luke tells us they broke bread together —probably meaning a combination of enjoying fellowship meals together, and sharing in the Lord's Supper. They also prayed together.

Judging by the language Luke uses, the early Christians no longer thought about their life in Jerusalem being regulated by the times when sacrifices were offered in the temple (Jesus had brought the need for sacrifices to an end). Instead they thought in terms of the times of prayer. Since the temple was by far the largest gathering space in the city, they met together there. They even seem to have had a preferred area of the temple (members of your church are not the first to sit in the same pew every service!). It must have been

[1] *Ibid.*, pp. 13-18.

quite a 'huddle' in the Colonnade of Solomon where they met (Acts 3:11; 5:12).

When we analyze the various dimensions of this addiction—their love to worship God, to be taught from his word, to praise their Lord, to pray—it is clear that it was not worship as such they loved—that would have been idolatry—but its purpose (to praise God). And the effect was startling—and three dimensional:

(i) 'awe came upon every soul' (Acts 2:43);

(ii) they had 'favour with the people' (Acts 2:47); and

(iii) 'the Lord added to their number day by day those who were being saved' (Acts 2:47).

The first two led naturally to the third. It is what happens when a church really is a church.

We will return to this theme of worship. But for the moment we should take a sneak preview at what happened next in the Jerusalem church. It is related to the sense of awe that marked them (Acts 2:43).

In Kenneth Grahame's famous book *The Wind in the Willows* he describes how Rat and Mole are gliding on the river and have an encounter with the 'supernatural.' Rat says to Mole:

> 'This is the place of my song-dream, the place the music played to me,' whispered the Rat, as if in a trance. 'Here, in this holy place, here if anywhere, surely we shall find Him!'
>
> Then suddenly the Mole felt a great Awe fall upon him, an awe that turned his muscles to water, bowed his head, and rooted his feet to the ground. It was no panic terror—indeed he felt wonderfully at peace and happy—but it was an awe that smote him and, without seeing, he knew it could only mean some august Presence was very, very near. With difficulty he turned to look for his friend, and saw him at his side cowed, stricken, and trembling violently …
>
> 'Rat!' he found breath to whisper, shaking. 'Are you afraid?'
>
> 'Afraid?' murmured the Rat, his eyes shining with unutterable

love. 'Afraid! Of *Him*? O, never, never! And yet—and yet—O, Mole, I am afraid.'

Then the two animals, crouching to the earth, bowed their heads and did worship.[1]

Sadly, what Kenneth Grahame had in view in this passage was man's sense of awe at Nature (capital 'N'!) since what Rat and Mole were hearing were the pipes of Pan, the pagan nature god. But if that could be true in the imagination of an author influenced by the Romantic movement, how much more true should it be in the church's worship of the God who has made himself known in Jesus Christ?

Later in Acts, following God's judgment on Ananias and his wife Sapphira for their reputation-seeking hypocrisy, Luke stretches our thinking by juxtaposing two paradoxical statements:

Acts 5:13: 'None of the rest dared join them …'

But then in the very next verse:

Acts 5:14: 'And more than ever believers were added to the Lord, multitudes of both men and women.'

That is real church. Outsiders will feel they are not really fit to join. And yet at the same time the displays of God's life-transforming grace in the fellowship awaken in them a deep longing for what they see—perhaps even with a little jealousy sometimes. The result is they are irresistibly drawn to Christ and all the blessings enjoyed in the fellowship of his church.

Yes, loving your church is a healthy addiction. And the Spirit wants to make it contagious.

---

[1] Kenneth Grahame, *The Wind in the Willows* (1908, repr. New York: Barnes and Noble, 2005), pp. 86-87.

5

Have You Ever Arrived at Church?

or

Worship

Have you ever arrived at church?

That may seem a strange question in a book like this. After all it would be surprising if anyone reading these pages had never been to church.

But there is more to the question than meets the eye.

Sometimes Christians today speak about the worship in their church in a way previous generations would have found strange and incomprehensible. I have heard ministers say things like: 'Expert church analysts have told us that, while there are weaknesses in our church, our worship is not one of them. In fact, they told us that the quality of our morning worship is outstanding.' So in this culture to ask the question 'Have you ever gone to worship?' seems naive, to say the least.

In the interests of full disclosure, my heart always sinks when I hear this kind of statement. Two thoughts immediately come to mind. The first, which will only make sense in the light of the previous chapter, is 'Why judge the quality by *morning* worship?' The second is this: 'Who do you think you are, church analyst, to assess the quality of worship?' In fact, the claim to give an expert assessment of a church's worship reveals a great deal. It almost always mistakes the means for the end, assessing only the external (the quality of the music, eloquence of the preaching). That we can assess, but not the internal—the hearts of the worshippers.

Good vehicles for worship are a blessing; but the only expert assessor of the quality of our worship is the Lord himself, before whom every heart is open, who 'is a consuming fire' (Heb. 12:29). If there is a way of assessing the quality of our worship, therefore, it is the degree to which we bring it 'with reverence and awe' (Heb. 12:28). Otherwise it may be that the object of our worship is no longer the Lord but our own worship of him. For true worshippers are not conscious of worship so much as they are of God and his presence.

If this is the case, then there is a difference between 'going to church' and 'arriving at church.'

Isaiah certainly thought so. From the beginning of his prophecy he exposes false worship masquerading as the true. God has 'had enough' of it (Isa. 1:11). It has 'become a burden to me,' he says (1:14). That may sound like the attitude we might have. But in this case it is God's attitude to going to church. He does not want to be present to witness the sham.

Yet none of this prepares us for what Isaiah describes a few chapters later, in what is by any measure one of the high points of the Bible: Isaiah chapter 6. It describes a day Isaiah went from his house to the temple in Jerusalem, but this time he 'arrived at church.' He found himself in the heavenly temple and experienced true worship. He would never be the same again. You never can be, after you have met with God in worship.

Isaiah had 'gone to church' all his life. He was 'Isaiah of Jerusalem.' By definition as a devout prophet of God he would have been frequently at the temple and experienced its many services.

But this day was different.

It was not that he was better prepared for worship than ever before. It was certainly not because he felt he had attained high levels of holiness that he had a unique spiritual experience. If you were to ask him, 'Was there anything that led you to expect this—an intimation that something special was about to happen?' his answer would probably have been: 'Nothing! I could never have predicted what happened that day. It was in the year King Uzziah died—I expected nothing.'

If after his experience Isaiah had made his way to the home of 'Benjamin' his Jerusalem friend, perhaps the conversation might have gone something like this:

Isaiah: Benjamin, may I sit down for a minute? I need to tell you something. I feel undone, as if I were coming to pieces, overwhelmed. I don't know whether to weep or to sing for joy. I am devastated and yet I feel exhilarated. Benjamin, I am a man of unclean lips.

Benjamin: Sit down, dear friend. What's happened? Can I get you something to drink? Are you unwell? Have you been overdoing things? Did you say you have unclean lips? No, dear friend! Not you! You are the last man in this city with unclean lips—you are our best preacher! Let's have no more of this talk. You are overtaxing yourself, my friend. These are difficult days for you. I think you may have overdone it. Just sit quietly for a moment.

Isaiah (pleadingly): But Benjamin—I feel I have been to temple worship today for the very first time in my life! I saw it—I mean, real worship! I heard worship: I tasted worship; I can't explain it, Benjamin, but feel I can never be the same again. Worship can never be the same again. And I long to sense the presence of God like that again and again!

We will see later that there is something in Isaiah 1–5 that prepares us for chapter 6. But here we should pause on this great moment. The person who has tasted what Isaiah did will never be the same again. He will know that what he needs in order to live a strong God-centred, Christ-honouring, Spirit-filled life is not a series of practical tips about how to become a happier, more-together, prosperous person. He will have tasted something much more pro-found, indeed much more devastating, than that—and yet at the same time far more satisfying—the presence of the Lord in his holiness and love.

What does it mean, then, to worship? If Isaiah's experience is a guide, then worship always involves:

1. The glory of God

What did you think or say at the end of this week's service? Strange, isn't it, that the most important aspect of worship is often the most forgotten? We 'liked' this or that part of the service; we didn't 'appreciate' another part because it didn't 'do much' for us.

Did it never cross our minds to ask if God was glorified? Did I come, and take part in the service as though worship was for my benefit? Perhaps that is why I didn't 'enjoy' it. For all of us surely know that 'Man's chief end is to glorify God and to enjoy him for ever.'[1] But perhaps you didn't really go in order to meet with God, and to worship and glorify him. Nothing took you by surprise; nothing overwhelmed you. To tell the truth you were a little 'underwhelmed.'

But God is overwhelming. He is the Creator of the universe. And he is the Lord of history. And he is the Saviour of sinners.

When Isaiah went into the temple, he had a vision of this God in all his glory:

> In the year that King Uzziah died I saw the Lord sitting upon a throne, high and lifted up; and the train of his robe filled the temple.

Isaiah felt that the place filled with a sense of God's presence. The temple itself seemed bigger inside than it looked from the outside. The overpowering sense of the infinite God of the universe felt as though he was concentrating his presence in one place. He filled the

---

[1] The Shorter Catechism, Question 1.

space and yet he could not be contained by it. So great was this sense of God that Isaiah could almost feel the train of his robe flowing down into the temple. He felt small, almost suffocated as it seemed to fill up more and more space. The pressure of the presence of God now seemed to be coming towards him, almost drowning him.

Of course this is what people experience in times of revival. But not only then. God still comes to church like that.

I remember when I was a teenager two of my friends went to a service at which Dr Martyn Lloyd-Jones was to be the preacher. In fact they were courting so (even as a youngster) I realized there was something inappropriate about gate-crashing! But I met one of them the next day. 'What was last night like?' I asked. The reply? 'He preached on the destruction of Dagon (1 Sam. 5). I felt as though the building was going to collapse!'

That was exactly what Isaiah felt: 'The foundations of the thresholds shook at the voice of him who called' (Isa. 6:4).

But what, exactly, did Isaiah experience?

2. *The sovereignty of God*

He saw God 'sitting upon a throne, high and lifted up.'

The church is not a democracy. It is the manifestation of a kingdom. Its King is glorious and exalted, surrounded by attendants of massive impressiveness. Whenever we hear the words—or words like them—'Let us worship God,' we are being invited to meet with him.

Scripture dates the great experiences of God's servants in different ways. But this particular service has a most unusual date: 'the year that king Uzziah died.'

Uzziah has been aptly described as the king who had a 'glorious reign with a ghastly end.'[1] Here is the explanation:

---

[1] George Adam Smith, *The Book of Isaiah* (8th ed., London: Hodder & Stoughton, 1893), p. 59.

In Jerusalem he [Uzziah] made engines, invented by skilful men, to be on the towers and the corners, to shoot arrows and great stones. And his fame spread far, for he was marvellously helped, till he was strong.

But when he was strong, he grew proud, to his destruction. For he was unfaithful to the LORD his God and entered the temple of the LORD to burn incense on the altar of incense. But Azariah the priest went in after him, with eighty priests of the Lord who were men of valour, and they withstood King Uzziah and said to him, 'It is not for you, Uzziah, to burn incense to the LORD, but for the priests the sons of Aaron, who are consecrated to burn incense. Go out of the sanctuary, for you have done wrong, and it will bring you no honour from the LORD God.' Then Uzziah was angry. Now he had a censer in his hand to burn incense, and when he became angry with the priests, leprosy broke out on his forehead in the presence of the priests in the house of the LORD, by the altar of incense. And Azariah the chief priest and all the priests looked at him, and behold, he was leprous in his forehead! And they rushed him out quickly, and he himself hurried to go out, because the LORD had struck him. And King Uzziah was a leper to the day of his death, and being a leper lived in a separate house, for he was excluded from the house of the LORD. And Jotham his son was over the king's household, governing the people of the land.

Now the rest of the acts of Uzziah, from first to last, Isaiah the prophet the son of Amoz wrote. And Uzziah slept with his fathers, and they buried him with his fathers in the burial field that belonged to the kings, for they said, 'He is a leper.' And Jotham his son reigned in his place. (2 Chron. 26:15-23)

God had been teaching Isaiah not to trust in the power of leaders no matter how great (how naive we still are!). But now he was showing him that in days of great crisis and disappointment, behind the scenes of time the throne of heaven was still occupied. God never vacates it.

This reality lies at the heart of worship. It is the reason it has such a recalibrating effect on our lives. None of us sees clearly. We constantly misinterpret reality. We live in a world where the price tags on the items on offer have been mixed up. As A. W. Tozer once wrote, what we need most of all is 'a baptism of clear seeing.' Only in God's light do we see light (Psa. 36:9). We come into his presence, we bow 'before Jehovah's awful throne,'[1] and stability returns. No matter who we are, or what is happening in our lives, God reigns. Meeting with him re-centres us on the One who is on the throne at the centre of heaven and, indeed, the centre of the universe.

3. *The holiness of God*

The strange and wonderful creatures (described here as seraphim, 'burning ones') who appear to Isaiah to fly above the Lord like ethereal attendants ('above' only because he is seated on the throne). Memorably they call out to one another in the words of a perpetual antiphony:

> Holy, holy, holy, is the LORD of hosts;
> The whole earth is full of his glory!

This is the only place in the Old Testament where the seraphim appear. It is also the only place in the Old Testament where we find a double repetition—'Holy, holy, holy …'

The Hebrew language in which the Old Testament was written works differently from English—quite apart from using a different script and being read from the right hand side of the page to the left! Classical biblical Hebrew uses repetition for the sake of emphasis. So, for example, God told Adam not to eat of the fruit of the tree of the knowledge of good and evil, because 'in the day that you eat of it *you shall surely die*' (Gen. 2:16-17). The emphatic 'you shall *surely* die' translates Hebrew which literally means '*dying* you shall *die.*'

Most of us are unconsciously familiar with this because of the way Jesus used repetition for the sake of emphasis, '*Truly, truly* I say

---

[1] John Wesley's arrangement of Isaac Watts' metrical version of Psalm 100.

to you …' It is as if he is saying, 'All my words are true—but this is a truth to which you must pay special attention.'

But Isaiah 6:3 is the only place in the Old Testament where a repetition for the sake of emphasis is itself repeated. It is an expression of the blazing intensity of God's holiness.

Isaiah *hears* this emphatic repetition of the seraphim proclaiming and extolling God's holiness. But he also *sees* it reflected in their posture.

They have six wings. With two of them they fly. With two of them they cover their feet (is this a sign that they uncover them only when their King bids them to fly in obedience to his command?). But what of the other two wings? With them they cover their faces.

'Of course,' we say, 'they are in the presence of the Holy One.'

True. But they are holy too—truly, permanently holy. They have never sinned. Thomas Binney (1798–1874) wrote of this in his magnificent hymn 'Eternal Light':

> Eternal Light! Eternal Light!
> How pure the soul must be
> When, placed within Thy searching sight,
> It shrinks not, but with calm delight
> Can live, and look on Thee.
>
> The spirits that surround Thy throne
> May bear the burning bliss;
> But that is surely theirs alone,
> Since they have never, never known
> A fallen world like this.

True. But perhaps not the whole truth. For Isaiah's vision suggests that there is a sense in which *created holiness* cannot 'bear the burning bliss.' The seraphim cannot gaze directly on uncreated, eternal, infinite, divinely intense holiness. The holiness of any creature, including the ethereal seraphim, is dependent, secondary, submissive, worshipping rather than independent and self sufficient.

Perhaps this is why the seraphim engage in such repetition. Perhaps, after all, it is not merely repetition as such. There is nothing repetitive (repeat, nothing!) about the worship of God. Our words can never mean simply and exactly the same every time we use them. We better understand the seraphim as they exclaim 'holy art thou' in their worship, if we grasp that every time they utter the praise of God and reflect on his holiness they experience an ever fresh sense of what that word means as they peer through their wings at his glory. Perhaps we are meant to read:

> Holy art Thou!
> O—how amazing Thy holiness is—
> Truly, holy art Thou …

I have often watched a young man standing at the front of a church bursting with emotion as his bride makes her way down the aisle towards him. You can often sense that he feels that it is impossible that any man has, or ever could, love any woman the way he feels he loves this woman.

But the young man knows almost nothing! Ten, twenty, thirty, fifty years later, and after saying ten thousand times 'you are the one I love'—then he will know better what his vows of love meant.

Is it like that for the seraphim as they gaze on the beauty of God's holiness? Peter tells us that the angels in heaven long to explore the mystery of the atonement—in which a holy God pardons sinners in a way that is utterly consistent with his holiness (1 Pet. 1:10-12). Does this suggest that when the antiphonal praise is rehearsed now in heaven there is an intensity, an understanding, a sense of awe, and amazement, a depth of worship in the words 'Holy, holy, holy' that expresses a new level and experience of seraphic worship?

And can it be like that for us too?

4. Sensing sin, tasting pardon

When God comes to church, he leaves nothing behind. He does not come dressed in only some of his attributes. Likewise, our worship involves seeing and sensing God as he really is. And so Isaiah begins to see God in his true light. But he also begins to see man—and especially himself—in his true colours. The manifestation of God's holiness carries with it the expression of his holy judgment. The temple itself is shaken; the prophet himself is shaken (he was not the last person to experience this. It is not something limited to the Old Testament. See Acts 4:31). Isaiah cries out in three staccato statements: 'Woe is me!' 'I am lost!' 'My lips are unclean.' Each of them carries its own special significance.

Isaiah feels himself 'lost.' The Hebrew word means something like 'ruined' or 'devastated.' Its root is a verb that means to be silent—like the awful hush that follows a disaster before panic breaks out. Isaiah feels as if he were disintegrating before God.

> The spirits that surround Thy throne
> May bear the burning bliss;

but Isaiah cannot.

We dread this; it suggests losing control of our own lives. But we also need it precisely for that reason. We want to have our lives—in modern parlance—'together'—under our own control. But the truth is that we are malformed. We can only 'get it together' in an artificial way by the employment of this world's various brands of superglue. By contrast what God does—yes even to a great man like Isaiah (perhaps *especially* to such a man)—is to take us to pieces and then reconstruct us. That is a recurring pattern in the Bible. For some it takes place through the long and slow process of God's providential working. It was thus for Jacob; it was so for Joseph. For others it happens in worship. That was so for Isaiah. That was the reason why, *as a prophet*, he needed to feel that his lips were unclean.

Earlier we imagined Isaiah visiting his friend Benjamin after this experience. How could this man, of all people in Jerusalem, say he had unclean lips? Simple, really. He had heard seraphim pronounce the word 'Holy' in a way he knew he never had.

David Garrick (perhaps the greatest English actor of the eighteenth century) once said—although he was no friend of Christianity —'I would give a hundred guineas to be able to say "Oh!" like [George] Whitefield' the evangelist. Whitefield, he added, could move an audience to either weeping or rejoicing simply by the way he could pronounce the word 'Mesopotamia.'[1] What Whitefield was to Garrick the seraphim were to Isaiah. Their seraphic pronunciation of the word 'holy' must have seemed to bring out all the richness and intensity of its meaning—so that Isaiah realized that his lips had never spoken properly of God, or worshipped him truly.

Perhaps the point Isaiah makes would be even clearer if his words were transcribed, 'I am a man of "unclean" lips.'

With what do you associate the cry 'unclean! unclean!'? It was the cry of the leper, simultaneously a confession of his condition and a warning to others that he was unclean.[2] Everyone familiar with Isaiah knows that he is the best preacher in Jerusalem. His lips are pure. They are his strength! But this is exactly the point. It was when he had grown strong that Isaiah's king, Uzziah, had grown proud and was struck down with leprosy. Had Isaiah been damningly critical of, as well as deeply disappointed in him? Now he is brought to his knees to confess: 'I have leprosy on my lips! "Unclean, unclean!"'

Worship in the presence of God has the power to undeceive us, doesn't it? We admit our weaknesses—and that is where we think sin lurks most influentially. But here we learn that this is not the case. Sin's most sinister work is in the way it weaves itself so insidiously

[1] Arnold Dallimore, *George Whitefield* (Edinburgh: Banner of Truth Trust, 1980), vol. 2, p. 530.

[2] Cf. the use of 'unclean' in Lev. 13:45, 46.

into our strengths, our abilities, into the very gifts of nature and of grace that God has given to us. Therein lies the terrible secret, and the sobering and shattering truth. Now Isaiah is discovering that he can only be reconstructed to be fit to speak for God when he has learned that the very instrument God will use must confess its own sin and be cleansed.

This explains why he cries out 'Woe is me!'

Isaiah chapter 6 is justly famous. But for that reason we tend to read it in isolation from the rest of the book. But the significance of at least one statement Isaiah makes comes home with full force only if we read it in context, from the beginning of the prophecy.

The Hebrew people seem to have loved numbers, design, shape, and arrangement in their narratives. Thus, for example, the Bible is full of threes and fours, sixes and sevens. And *seven* was an especially important number. God created in six days and rested on the seventh—it was almost as if the number seven were 'written in' to the nature of things; it signified completeness, finality, and fulness. For that reason any reference to a series of six created an anticipation of a seventh—the climax.

With this in mind, look back through Isaiah chapter 5, and notice Isaiah's list of woes upon a variety of sins and sinners:

Woe 1: Isaiah 5:8

> Woe to those who join house to house,
>   who add field to field,
> until there is no more room,
>   and you are made to dwell alone
>   in the midst of the land.

Woe 2: Isaiah 5:11

> Woe to those who rise early in the morning,
>   that they may run after strong drink,

> who tarry late into the evening
>> as wine inflames them!

Woe 3: Isaiah 5:18

> Woe to those who draw iniquity with cords of falsehood,
>> who draw sin as with cart ropes,

Woe 4: Isaiah 5:20

> Woe to those who call evil good and good evil,
> who put darkness for light and light for darkness,
> who put bitter for sweet and sweet for bitter!

Woe 5: Isaiah 5:21

> Woe to those who are wise in their own eyes,
>> and shrewd in their own sight!

Woe 6: Isaiah 5:22

> Woe to those who are heroes at drinking wine,
>> and valiant men in mixing strong drink,

What next? Will there be a seventh and final woe? Against whom will Isaiah pronounce it? Here is the answer:

Woe 7: Isaiah 6:5

> Woe is me! For I am lost;
>> for I am a man of unclean lips,
>>> and I dwell in the midst of a people of unclean lips;
>> for my eyes have seen the King, the Lord of hosts!

One of the first lessons anyone ever taught me as a young Christian was this: the nearer you come to the Lord the more sinful you will feel yourself to be. It cannot be any other way. Never lose sight of that. What is more, the whole Christian life involves an ever repeated cycle of discovering fresh layers of sin to be dealt with and fresh supplies of forgiveness and cleansing. And in the process of the successive cycles there may be major incursions of heart-revelation.

These are designed to bring us to see how deep-dyed sin has been in our hearts but that there is correspondingly deep pardon and cleansing available for us in Christ. Isaiah 6 describes one of those moments, indeed *the* moment, in Isaiah's life when he made this rediscovery.

There is a law of the spiritual universe illustrated graphically here: *it is only when we confess our sin that we experience forgiveness.*

This principle is logical, really. The person who has no sense of sin does not feel any need for forgiveness. Why should we? This was one of the problems Jesus had with his contemporaries. They were blind, but thought they could see. Of course they felt no need of Jesus as the Light of the world, or to follow him so that they would not walk in darkness.[1] They thought they were already in the light. But, as Jesus said elsewhere, if the light that is in us is darkness— how great is that darkness! (Matt. 6:23).

A curious discomfort seems to characterize many Christians. At the time of the Reformation, leaders like John Calvin and John Knox were deeply concerned that in the worship services there would be a time when the people could together confess their sins. What is curious in this context is that church leaders who share this desire and want to implement it by introducing a corporate confession of sin sometimes meet with stubborn resistance. Often that comes from well-meaning evangelical people who say 'But we don't confess sin like this, using words that someone has already written down for us.' Yet the same people love to sing such words as these:

> Naked, come to Thee for dress;
> > Helpless, look to Thee for grace;
> Foul, I to the fountain fly;
> > Wash me, Saviour, or I die.[2]

---

[1] See John 8:12.

[2] From the hymn 'Rock of Ages, cleft for me' by Augustus Montague Toplady (1740–48).

Why would we think that what we *sing* with deep emotion carries a sincerity that what we *say* doesn't?

But to return to Isaiah. Notice some of the details of what happened next.

A seraph goes to the altar of sacrifice, takes a pair of tongs that lie beside it, and with them he lifts up a piece of burning coal. He now flies in the direction of Isaiah.

Isaiah is about to experience forgiveness and pardon. It comes from the altar of sacrifice.

The prophet is learning two lessons:

Lesson one: Pardon for sin comes at a price.

There is no forgiveness without sacrifice, no pardon without a penalty for sin being paid. As the author of Hebrews would later put it, 'without the shedding of blood there is no forgiveness of sins' (Heb. 9:22). What happened on that altar was a picture of what Jesus would do on the cross. In fact, John later says that Isaiah was able to write his prophecy because he 'saw' Christ's glory and spoke about him (John 12: 41).

But there is a second lesson we must not miss.

Lesson two: See what the seraph does!

He picks the coal out of the altar fire with the tongs. Then he transfers it to his hand. It seems that seraphim have hands as well as wings; and those hands are able to bear heat beyond the tolerance level of any man or woman. But do you see what happens now? The seraph touches Isaiah's lips and mouth with the burning coal!

Excruciating pain! The sight is almost unbearable. Perhaps you have a vivid imagination and can envisage this. You find yourself clenching your fists, tightening your whole body, ready to close your eyes at the sight and put your fingers to your ears to protect them from the shrieks that will issue from Isaiah's lips. They are, surely, about to be silenced forever. The burned lips and mouth of the prophet Isaiah will never again be able to speak for God.

But no. The seraph says, 'This has touched your lips; your guilt is taken away, and your sin atoned for' (Isa. 6:7). Oh blessed pain! Excruciating joy! For the tongue that has been scalded by grace scales the heights of grandeur in praise. Where sin once reigned, grace now reigns.[1]

Being forgiven is for some people by far the most painful, even excruciating, experience of life. To discover you are a sinner, and that your sin is entwined in what you think of as your virtues, strengths, good qualities, and special gifts—to discover that these are the areas of life in which sin grips you, blinds you, condemns you—what personal devastation that produces. Isaiah's cry, 'I am *lost*,' is the right word. Everything we counted as gain now needs to be burned away as so much dross, and counted as loss.[2]

But, what a glorious loss this is when it leads us to the Saviour! This is worship.

And this 'order of worship' is surprisingly like the pattern of our church services, or should be. For the liturgy that leads us into the presence of God and then discloses our sin in order to lead us to his grace and pardon then prepares us to hear his voice in his word.

5. The sermon

We will think further about God's word in the next chapter. But notice here that, following the praise, adoration and confession of God's holiness and human sin that Isaiah has heard and shared, and the word of absolution he has heard with all the relief to conscience it brings … now comes the sermon. Now God speaks.

God speaks in his word. But he does not mention Isaiah by name. He seems to speak to the whole congregation (are we meant

---

[1] Cf. Romans 5:21.

[2] As Saul of Tarsus was brought—very painfully—to see: Philippians 3:4-9.

to envisage Isaiah surrounded by other worshippers although they have not been mentioned?). The point of the sermon is this: God is calling for someone to go in his name to serve him in the world: 'Whom shall I send and who will go for us?' (Isa. 6:8).

'Lord, look over here!' Isaiah cries out. 'Here I am! Send me! I will go for you.'

It would not surprise me if Isaiah cried out like this in the middle of the service. I have seen that happen on occasion as the word of God—preached to the whole congregation—has so taken grip on one person that they have lost all sense of being in a crowd, and even of the difference between what is being said from the pulpit and what is being spoken by God right into their hearts. The result is that they speak out loud their innermost thoughts. God's voice is sometimes heard in preaching in this real, powerful, and deeply personal way. I feel he is speaking to me as if I were the only person present. And there seems to be nothing about me that is hidden from him.

Did Isaiah simply make his way to the temple, did he just 'come to church' on that never-to-be-forgotten day in the same way he usually did? Like other days there was a good congregation. He found his place in the crowd. But he did not remain hidden in the crowd. God knew exactly where he was.

Isaiah could never be the same again. That was obviously, dramatically true. But it is always true when we come to church to meet with God. We come as we are, but we never leave the way we came. We have met with God, discovered again our sinfulness, tasted his pardon, responded to his word—or we have ignored him. We have confessed our sins and been forgiven—or we have left his presence like the Pharisee in Jesus' parable, content but unpardoned.[1]

God never leaves us in church in the same condition in which he found us when we came to worship (or, alas, if we came *not* to

---

[1] Luke 18:9-14.

worship). His presence touches us, his word comes to us, teaches, convicts, transforms and equips us, and we leave humbled, pardoned, and renewed, Or, we leave with our hearts and minds a little more hardened. Just as the sun that warms produces growth but also may harden the soil, so our hearts may be converted or hardened by the word of God, its exposure of our sin, and its gospel message of forgiveness for all who will say 'I am unclean … pardon me.'

That was the message Isaiah was called to proclaim to his contemporaries. It was Jesus' message too.[1]

Were there others around Isaiah? Did they see the Lord high and lifted up, hear the seraphim praise God for his holiness, realize their sinfulness, experience pardon, find challenge and direction in the 'sermon,' and leave renewed? No doubt there were others around him who saw nothing, felt nothing, and heard nothing—and left thinking (and perhaps even saying) 'There was nothing there for me today!'

It is said that on one occasion William Wilberforce (so instrumental in the abolition of the slave trade) took his close friend William Pitt the Younger (one of the most famous of British Prime Ministers) to hear William Romaine preach. At least three 'Williams' were in church that day! William Romaine was one of the finest preachers of his generation, with a burden to point his hearers to Jesus Christ. As they left, William Wilberforce felt his heart was burning with the truth and glory of the message he had just heard. But as he and the third William engaged in conversation it was as though Romaine and Wilberforce had been in one place and William Pitt somewhere entirely different. Wilberforce, the committed Christian, felt his heart sink as Pitt said, in total mystification, 'Wilberforce, what was Romaine going on about today?'

Perhaps in the same way, others who were in the temple at exactly the same time as Isaiah went home for their meal, and as they sat

---

[1] Isaiah 6:9, 10. Compare Jesus' teaching about his parables in Matthew 13:13-15.

down at table said: 'Sad about Uzziah, isn't it? Why doesn't God prevent that kind of thing if he is all-powerful? Sometimes I wonder if there's really any point to going up to the temple.'

Yes, sadly, it is possible—all too possible—to 'come to church' and yet never 'arrive at worship.'

Years ago, the president of the seminary in which I taught was planning a tour of the sites of 'The Seven Churches of Revelation'—visiting the locations of the ancient churches mentioned in the first three chapters of the Book of Revelation. I asked him 'Are you going to Patmos (the rocky island in the Aegean Sea where John was exiled and where he had the vision he recorded in Revelation). 'No,' came the reply; 'I asked the tour company people and they said "There's nothing to see there."' Instinctively I responded, 'Tell that to the apostle John!'

Yet it is true that you could have been on Patmos on that never-to-be-forgotten Lord's day towards the end of the first century AD and seen nothing. By contrast, John was 'in the Spirit on the Lord's day' (Rev. 1:10). And he experienced heavenly worship.

It is still possible today to go to worship and be 'in the Spirit on the Lord's day' and sense the glory of the Lord among his people. And it is also possible simply to go to church and sense nothing.

How much we need the Holy Spirit if we are to worship in Spirit and truth (John 4:23)!

Thankfully, it is not too late to get into the service.

6

Are You Hearing Me?

or

The Bible

———

I n my childhood and all the way through my twenties, almost every church service I attended, began with the same solemn, but simple ritual. In some churches, as the congregation waited for the service to begin, a man would appear from some hidden room, carrying an enormous black 'pulpit' Bible. He would mount the pulpit steps, and carefully place it on the reading desk, ceremoniously open it and unfold markers in it that would sometimes fall over the front of the pulpit.

This man—known throughout Scotland as 'the Beadle'—would then come down the pulpit steps, and allow the minister to enter the pulpit. Then, in what always seemed a curious ritual to a youngster, many times the Beadle would follow the minister back up the steps, and close the door of the pulpit behind him, often moving the door catch so that the minister would be 'locked' into the pulpit. Then at the end of the service the whole process would be repeated in reverse order! Safely locked in—presumably it was a symbolic act to remind the minister that he was now 'locked in' to the task of leading the people together into the presence of God—then, and only then, would the minister say the words that have always had a powerful emotional effect on me: 'Let us worship God.'

The 'meaning' of the ritual was fairly obvious. And intriguingly the word 'beadle' is derived from the Old English *bydel* which meant someone who made a proclamation. Our beadles never spoke. But the ritual they enacted each week spoke for itself. In a way it was a more powerful proclamation than any words they might speak. It proclaimed: the Bible is God's word. He reveals his will in and through it. We live under its authority for all of life, including worship. Life should be lived, and worship should be conducted according to God's will, not ours. What is about to happen takes place under his lordship, according to his good pleasure made known to us in the Old and New Testaments. Therefore, woe betide the minister who does not submit to God's word and teach its message to his congregation!

I have not witnessed this ritual for many years now. Today it would probably be regarded as 'quaint,' not sufficiently informal. But it made the point with evocative symbolism. It impressed upon me the importance and the centrality of the word of God. The church lives under its authority.

In many churches we confess this when we become members. Take for example, this question from the membership covenant of a congregation to which I belonged: 'Do you believe the Scripture of the Old and New Testaments to be the written word of God, the only perfect rule of faith and practice?'

What does this mean? And why is it so important?

Self-descriptions

It is always interesting to discover how a church thinks about itself and its basic identity. Sometimes when I have had the opportunity to speak to elders in a congregation I have asked this question: 'How would you describe your church? What words would you use to express how you see yourselves—how would you summarize your identity as a church?'

I recall on one occasion receiving the answer 'We are a biblical church.' The answer to the follow-up question—'How would you define a biblical church?'—was revealing: 'A biblical church is *a church where the Bible is preached from the pulpit.*'

Now there should be no doubt about the importance and value of that. Churches are made or marred by what happens in the pulpit. But a biblical *church* is much more than one in which the Bible is preached. I have known churches no one would think of describing as 'biblical' where, nevertheless, the Bible has been preached. A biblical *church* is, surely, one in which the Bible gets out of the pulpit, as it were, and begins to move into the congregation, getting into our lives, changing us, challenging us, convicting us, motivating us, and pointing us to all the resources of God. There is little point in guarding the pulpit if that means we are locking God's word up inside it and refusing it entry into our life together as God's people and our individual and family lives as well. Sometimes such a church will be known as 'a teaching church.' But if so it needs to ask, 'What is the point of learning?' For the purpose of the Bible is not merely educational. It is transformational. This is why Jesus prayed for his disciples before his crucifixion, '*Sanctify* them in the truth; your word is truth' (John 17:17). His passion was to see the word of truth work out in lives of truth.

This theme was virtually the last topic about which the apostle Paul ever wrote.

When a Christian is conscious that his or her time left here is short, he or she will want to focus on saying the most important things of all to family and friends. That was true of the Lord Jesus.[1] It was also true of Paul. Thus, in his last letter to his young friend Timothy—which may have been his last letter ever—he places tremendous emphasis on the role of Scripture.

---

[1] As is evident in John's Gospel, chapters 13 to 17.

All who desire to live a godly life in Christ Jesus will be persecuted, while evil people and impostors will go on from bad to worse, deceiving and being deceived. But as for you, continue in what you have learned and have firmly believed, knowing from whom you learned it and how from childhood you have been acquainted with the sacred writings, which are able to make you wise for salvation through faith in Christ Jesus. All Scripture is breathed out by God and profitable for teaching, for reproof, for correction, and for training in righteousness, that the man of God may be competent, equipped for every good work.

I charge you in the presence of God and of Christ Jesus, who is to judge the living and the dead, and by his appearing and his kingdom: preach the word; be ready in season and out of season; reprove, rebuke, and exhort, with complete patience and teaching.

(2 Tim. 3:12–4:2)

We are all interested in *profit*. We want to know that what we do is not a waste of time or effort. So what profit should I expect from the Bible? And how should I expect to receive that profit in reading it for myself and in hearing it explained and expounded?

1. Salvation

First of all, the Bible—in this instance, the Old Testament—taught Timothy how to find salvation through faith in Jesus Christ.

We do not know all the details of how this happened in Timothy's life, except that his mother and grandmother taught him the Bible.[1] Perhaps their teaching went something like this:

Right from the beginning, the Bible is full of promises that God will rescue his people. The first of these promises is in Genesis 3:15, where God promised Eve that there would come a day when her seed would crush the head of the serpent who had tempted and trapped her and her husband. In that triumph the serpent would crush the heel of her descendant.

---

[1] Timothy was the son of a 'mixed marriage.' His mother, Eunice, was Jewish but his father was a Gentile (Acts 16:1).

That promise was developed and extended when God told Abraham that in his seed the nations of the earth would be blessed (Gen. 12:1, 2).

But how? Slowly the story unfolded. God would raise up a Prophet like Moses, a Priest after the order of Melchizedek, a King who would be greater than David. The Son of Man would appear (Deut. 18:15; Psa. 110:4; Psa. 72:1ff; Dan. 7:13, 14).

Alongside this was an entire worship system that was centred on sacrifices being made for the sins of the people. Animals who had never sinned were substituted for men and women who had—and in the process the animals' lives were forfeited.

These sacrifices went on day after day, year after year. Those who had eyes to see and faith to understand must have realized that *animal sacrifices* could not make sufficient atonement for *human sin*. They must be symbols, interim substitutes, pointers to a greater sacrifice. At the high point of this divine revelation, Isaiah wrote about that sufficient sacrifice when he described the mysterious figure of the Servant of the Lord:

> Surely he has borne our griefs
>   and carried our sorrows;
> yet we esteemed him stricken,
>   smitten by God, and afflicted.
> But he was pierced for our transgressions;
>   he was crushed for our iniquities;
> upon him was the chastisement that brought us peace,
>   and with his wounds we are healed.
> All we like sheep have gone astray;
>   we have turned every one to his own way;
> and the Lord has laid on him
>   the iniquity of us all. (Isa. 53:4-6)

The promises and the sacrifices were parallel lines of revelation that would eventually meet in the person and work of the Lord Jesus.

Sometimes people stumble on the Bible. I remember hearing of a famous British actor working in New York and finding himself overcome with a desire to read it. Failing to find one in his hotel room he went out of the hotel and tried to find a shop that sold Bibles. Eventually he found one, devoured its message like a hungry man, and became a Christian.

Others, perhaps most of us, first encounter the Bible in a significant way not so much by reading it for ourselves but when we 'see' its message lived out in someone else's life. We may not make the connection at first. But then it dawns on us.

And then there are others who have the privilege of hearing the Bible read in their home and seeing it worked out in a father or mother. That was Timothy's story—and in his case it included his grandmother Lois. From his mother's knee, Timothy learned the great Bible stories. But something more was needed—he needed to know where the story-line of his mother's Bible stories reached its climax. Enter the apostle Paul.

Paul came to the area of Lystra where Timothy's family lived. He began to preach and seems to have continued to do so for some time (Acts 15:5-7). It was probably at this point that Timothy's mother and grandmother (whom Paul obviously knew) and perhaps Timothy himself had come to faith in Christ. This would explain why Paul refers to him as 'my true child in the faith' (1 Tim. 1:2) and 'my beloved child' (2 Tim. 1:2)—he was his spiritual father. Somewhere in this time period the Old Testament pictures of salvation began to make complete sense—now that he knew how the story had come to its climax in Jesus. He was the promised person; he was also the real sacrifice for sin. And Timothy had seen the effect of understanding this and believing in Jesus as Saviour and Lord in Paul's life and ministry.

My own experience was similar. I started to read the Bible when I was nine years old. Looking back now I marvel at the way that I did this diligently and daily for about five years without really 'seeing' its essential message. Then I met people whose lives seemed to connect with what I had been reading. To be honest, even as a young teenager, it came as a shock to realize that there is a difference between reading the Bible—even regularly—and discovering its message for yourself, seeing your need of salvation, and finding the forgiveness and new life it promises to everyone who believes in Christ.

2. The mouth of God[1]

How should we read the Bible? How do we go about?

Paul gives us an important clue when he writes that 'all Scripture is *breathed out* by God' (2 Tim. 3:16). Older Bible versions used to translate that as '*inspired* by God,' but the word Paul uses (*theopneustos*) expresses the idea that God has 'breathed out' Scripture, not that he 'breathes into' it. In other words, we should come to the Bible as if we were listening to God talking—because we are.

Jesus shared this view of the Bible. He indicates that in various ways. For example, when he was tempted by Satan in the wilderness, he not only quoted the words of the Bible as though they had the authority of God himself, he specifically refers to the words of Deuteronomy 8:3: 'Man shall not live by bread alone but by every word that comes from the mouth of God' (Matt. 4:4). In keeping with these words, Jesus thought about the Old Testament as God's 'mouth.'

People who know each other intimately can often communicate a great deal without speaking. But even if we say 'I know what you are thinking' we still think in terms of words. The wonder of Scripture is that the infinitely great God of the cosmos has 'breathed out' words to us. He made us as his image in order that we might be able to receive and understand his words. So, when we read the Bible, we say with Samuel, 'Speak, for your servant hears' (1 Sam. 3:10).

God *has spoken* in his word, the Bible. But he also *continues to speak* in and through it. At least that is how the Christians in the

[1] For a fuller discussion see Sinclair B. Ferguson, *From the Mouth of God* (Edinburgh: Banner of Truth Trust, 2014).

New Testament period saw things. Thus the author of Hebrews writes:

> And have you forgotten the exhortation that *addresses you* as sons?
> 'My son, do not regard lightly the discipline of the Lord,
> nor be weary when reproved by him.' (Heb. 12:5)

The author is quoting from the Old Testament, specifically from Proverbs 3:11-12. He quotes ancient words breathed out by God so long ago, but believes that in them he *addresses you*—first-century Christians (notice the present tense)—and therefore us as well.

This was how Isaiah prophesied Jesus would live:

> The Lord God has given me the tongue
> of those who are taught,
> that I may know how to sustain with a word
> him who is weary.
> Morning by morning he awakens;
> he awakens my ear
> to hear as those who are taught.
> The Lord God has opened my ear,
> and I was not rebellious;
> I turned not backward. (Isa. 50:4, 5)

This is how we too are to live and feed on God's word.

But what difference does the Bible make—if any—to our lives?

3. Transformation

While Paul stressed the inspiration of the Bible, he actually says more about its *effect* in our lives. Some people in our churches would become very upset (and rightly so) if a preacher told them that they could safely ignore large portions of Scripture. And yet if you were to ask them what difference those sections had made in their lives you might be greeted with an embarrassed silence. Doesn't it sound hollow to protest the full inspiration of the Bible but ignore parts of it? Doesn't that turn the Bible into an idea rather than a relevant, life-transforming message from the heavenly Father? So there is an important sense in which our conviction about the inspiration of the Bible is actually proved only by how much we allow it to influence our lives.

According to Paul, God's word operates at four different levels to do this:

> All Scripture is breathed out by God and profitable for *teaching*, for *reproof*, for *correction*, and for *training in righteousness*, that the man of God may be competent, equipped for every good work.

(i) Teaching

One of the most alarming effects of our fallen condition—and most difficult to accept—is that our minds are affected by sin. In some ways it is akin to loss of memory—the alarming element is that what we think of as the very instrument we use in order to remember something—our 'memory'—itself malfunctions.

Most of us trust our minds to operate properly. We feel sure we 'see things the way they really are.' But Scripture teaches differently. It explains that our minds have been darkened by sin—we can no longer think clearly about God, the world, or ourselves.

Of course we believe we can. That is precisely the problem.

One of my earliest memories of elementary school is of trying to convince the teacher that she had mis-spelled a word she had written on the board. We had been trained to spell using a book of spelling lists produced by the famous Australian educationalist Sir Fred Schonell. We thought we knew our spelling.

So, what was the word whose spelling I debated so hotly with our teacher? It was the word 'height.' I argued—I am embarrassed to say, confidently—that she had mis-spelled it. It is spelled 'hight' I insisted, since it is the noun related to the adjective 'high.' True, I would have fitted well into the late sixteenth century before there were such things as dictionaries, and therefore before spelling was regulated.[1] And I might have been given some points in a logic class, were there such a subject in elementary school. But even if my argument was a valid one, it was wrong! I was very sure of my thinking, clear in my logic, but, of course, very wrong in my spelling!

We can be similarly blind—and stubborn!—when it comes to spiritual realities. We are sure we are right, and that we know best. We may even be sure that so long as we do our best all will be well with God. But we need a teacher to instruct us and to bring us to acknowledge the truth—God's truth, God's view of our lives. Scripture does that.

First, Scripture explains that by nature our minds are both darkened and hardened (Rom. 1:21; Eph. 4:17-19). Jesus had underlined the same point. The light of the body, he said, is the eye. But if we have an eye disease, our whole body is in darkness. His application? If we think we live in the light—see things clearly—but the light within us is actually darkness, then how great that darkness is (cf. Matt. 6:22-23).

Because Scripture brings us teaching from God it illumines that darkness and helps us to see things clearly at last. However, it does not do this all on its own. Its laser beams remove the spiritual cataracts from our eyes only when they are directed by the heavenly ophthalmic surgeon, the Holy Spirit. That is why one of the first prayers we should learn by heart and use is from Psalm 119:18:

> Open my eyes, that I may behold
> Wondrous things out of your law.

---

[1] It may be worth noting in passing, since the present book employs British spelling, that this is the reason the American and British spelling of some words differs. It is not that British spelling is right and American spelling wrong (despite what is sometimes thought by people in the UK!). It is simply that in the two different contexts over time one spelling rather than the other was standardized. Authentic autographs of William Shakespeare suggest he himself used different spellings of his own name.

(ii) Reproof

Then, secondly, God's word is useful for *reproof.* The word 'reproof' carries with it the atmosphere of pain being inflicted!—a rebuke for errors and mistakes. Of course it hurts—we are sinners; being called in question is never pleasant. The word of God gets under our skin, probes our failures, and brings to the surface our sin.

We discover that the word of God is empowered to penetrate into the depths of our souls:

> For the word of God is living and active, sharper than any two-edged sword, piercing to the division of soul and of spirit, of joints and of marrow, and discerning the thoughts and intentions of the heart. (Heb. 4:12)

Jesus used similar language about the ministry of the Holy Spirit:

> And when he comes, he will convict the world concerning sin and righteousness and judgment: concerning sin, because they do not believe in me; concerning righteousness, because I go to the Father, and you will see me no longer; concerning judgment, because the ruler of this world is judged. (John 16:8-11)

In the first instance he was referring to the coming of the Spirit on the Day of Pentecost. If you read the account of what happened (in Acts 2:14-41) you will see that Jesus' words were a prophetic summary of the event. But this is also an ongoing ministry of the Spirit. He uses his word as a mirror of our souls to reveal the crevices in which sin continues to lurk in our lives. Thus the author of Hebrews continues:

> And no creature is hidden from his sight, but all are naked and exposed to the eyes of him to whom we must give account.
>
> (Heb. 4:13)

People with an episcopalian background are familiar with the words of the 'Collect for Purity' that in English at least goes back to Thomas Cranmer's Prayer Book in the reign of Edward VI:

> Almighty God,
> unto whom all hearts be open, all desires known,
> and from whom no secrets are hid:
> cleanse the thoughts of our hearts
> by the inspiration of thy Holy Spirit,
> that we may perfectly love thee,
> and worthily magnify thy holy name:
> through Christ our Lord. Amen.

The wonderful thing is that God does this through his word. He does not 'go public' with our sins, but quietly takes us aside and exposes them to us—in order for something spiritually new to take place in us. We should expect this. But if we resist it we will be refusing to allow the word of God to do its real work in our lives.

But in addition to teaching and rebuking, the Scriptures are also profitable for—

(iii) Correction

The word deconstructs us. It does so, not to destroy us, but to clear the ground, to deal with everything that distorts our lives and draws them away from the Lord and his blessing.

When I was a youngster the word 'correct' had an ominous and negative tone to it as far as I was concerned. It meant I had done something wrong and was being rebuked and might be liable to punishment. Being 'corrected' and being 'rebuked' amounted to the same thing! But the term Paul uses (*epanorthōsis*) has a much more positive ring to it—as the appearance of *orthōsis* might suggest even to an English reader. This word has the same Greek root as our words *ortho*paedic, *ortho*dontist, and yes *ortho*doxy. *Orthos* means straight, or upright. *Epanorthōsis* appears outside of the New Testament in the context of the healing of a broken bone. So, if *rebuking* involves the demolition of what is sinful, then *correction* involves the rebuilding, the straightening out of our lives and the reshaping of them into the image of Christ—which is, after all, God's purpose for us (Rom. 8:29).

This is what happens when God's word does God's work in our lives.

Think of little Zacchaeus coming down from the sycamore tree in response to the word of Jesus (Luke 19:1-10). What a twisted little man he was inwardly. He had feathered his own nest at the expense of others. He loved money more than people, and certainly more than he loved God. But now, through Jesus' word his sins were forgiven and his life transformed. The 'superglue' of the sin of greed was dissolving right before his neighbours' eyes. Instead of *taking*, he began to *give*. This was the 'corrected' version of Zacchaeus—and a very much more attractive person he was! His deformities were being healed. *That is what 'correction' means.*

At 6.00 a.m. one Monday morning in the summer of 1515, a theology professor in the new University of Wittenberg, having just completed a multi-semester course on the Psalms, began another series of lectures on Paul's letter to the Romans. It would last for three semesters. The students must have felt the hairs rise on the back of their necks as they heard the opening words of the lecture. For after, presumably, a brief prayer, their thirty-one year old professor, an Augustinian monk by the name of Martin Luther, applied to Paul's letter to the Romans some words that God had spoken to the prophet Jeremiah:[1]

> The sum and substance of this letter is: to pull down, to pluck up, and to destroy all wisdom and righteousness of the flesh (i.e. of whatever importance they may be in the sight of men and even in our own eyes) no matter how heartily and sincerely they may be

---

[1] See Jer. 1:9, 10: 'Then the Lord put out his hand and touched my mouth. And the Lord said to me, "Behold, I have put my words in your mouth. See, I have set you this day over nations and over kingdoms, to pluck up and to break down, to destroy and to overthrow, to build and to plant."'

practiced, and to implant, establish, and make large the reality of sin (however unconscious we may be of its existence).[1]

We could say the same thing about the whole Bible.

(iv) Training in righteousness.

The word of God is not only a hospital to heal us; it is also a gymnasium in which we are strengthened and equipped for service. It provides exercises that stretch us and build up our spiritual muscles; it thus trains and equips us to serve Christ.

When I was young, older Christians used an expression that is rarely heard today. They spoke about being 'in the word.' That is an expressive way of saying, 'let the word of Christ dwell in you richly' (Col. 3:16) to change, mould, and prepare you to serve the Lord. Paul's exhortation in his letter to the Colossians is exactly parallel to what he says to the Ephesians: 'Be filled with the Spirit' (Eph. 5:18). If we want to be the latter, we must do the former. We are filled with the Spirit as we drink in the word. The result? From one point of view it may seem relatively unspectacular—our lives will begin to bear the fruit of the Spirit (Gal. 5:22-23). But, in fact, *that* is a spectacular transformation. It means developing a Jesus-like character. Only thus do we become spiritually and morally 'competent, equipped for every good work' (2 Tim. 3:17).

Before we leave this passage we should notice some of the practical implications of its teaching for our life together in the church and for our own Bible study.

Guidelines for Bible study

There were, of course, no numbered verses or chapter divisions in Paul's letters. Unfortunately, the chapter break between 2 Timothy

---

[1] Martin Luther, *Lectures on Romans*, trans. Wilhelm Pauck (Philadelphia: Westminster Press, 1961), p. 3.

3 and 4 tends to obscure something important. If we rightly ignore it and read on we notice that, having written to Timothy about the usefulness of Scripture, he urges him to use it in these ways: he is to 'preach the word … reprove, rebuke, and exhort, with complete patience and teaching' (2 Tim. 4:2). He is echoing his own words.

Obviously these words have a special relevance to those in the church who preach. But they are also relevant to all of us who listen. We need to do all we can to make sure that all these elements are present in the church we attend, otherwise we may starve spiritually.

There is a message for preachers. Their calling in life is to do exactly what Paul says here. So if the congregation is not being carefully taught God's word; and if there is no element of rebuke, and correction, and equipping for service, then that fellowship needs another minister who will follow through with Paul's exhortation. It is as simple, serious, and important as that. Our own preachers may not be the best in the world; but that is not the issue. Rather it is whether there is enough instruction, feeding, challenging, and nurturing to transform our lives. If not we need to beware, because it does not take long for us to be so starved spiritually that we become sick and lose our appetite altogether.

But Paul's words also help us when we study the Bible together in groups. We need to understand that it is not having 'small groups' as such that strengthens the church. It is *what happens when we do have them*. There is a place for sitting around and sharing our lives as fellow Christians. But in small groups sometimes the problems actually arise when we open our Bibles!

Often in group Bible studies the question we ask is 'What is this passage saying to you as an individual?' The result is that we read the Bible looking, by and large, for something that strikes us as being relevant or applicable to our own lives at this moment. The result? We sometimes lose sight of what the passage we are studying is actually saying: we move too quickly to application. So Paul's words are very helpful to us because they give us some basic hints for reading and studying Scripture. He is telling us what the Bible as a whole, and each individual passage in particular, is *for*. And so we should always have the following thoughts in mind:

- The Bible is profitable for teaching. *What is the teaching, or doctrine, in this passage?*

- The Bible is profitable for rebuking. *What sins does this passage expose and rebuke?*

- The Bible is profitable for correction. *In what ways does this passage show us, positively, how to live for Christ? Does it tell us what and why and how to replace the old with the new?*

- The Bible is profitable for training in righteousness, to equip us for every good work. *How does this passage train and equip us? For what good work does it prepare us?*

Many years ago as a young minister I developed a kind of diagnostic tool to help people I knew think more clearly about Bible study. I called it 'The Ephesians Test' because of the first time I experimented with it.

A friend told me that he was having wonderful 'Quiet Times' (as periods of Bible study and prayer were sometimes called). I asked him what book of the Bible he was studying. 'Ephesians,' he replied. We were good friends and so I thought I would try out my diagnostic tool on him. I asked him this question:

Imagine that when you started reading Ephesians, I had given you a blank notebook, and asked you to record your reflections on each day's passage. Then imagine that at the end of the month you let me read what you had written. Would I find either:

(a) A fascinating account of your life during the past month, prompted by what you had read in Ephesians.

or

(b) A description of what Ephesians teaches, with some applications to your life, indicating what you need to learn, and how, by God's grace, Ephesians has shown you not only your sin but the riches of God's grace in Christ and the nature of the transformed life God calls and equips you to live.

My friend smiled. He immediately saw what I was asking. 'Oh,' he said, '(a)! No question!'

He admitted he had only the haziest idea of what Paul actually said in Ephesians—only the memory of an occasional verse. He certainly could not have told me what the message of Ephesians was, or given a simple outline of its teaching. His Bible study was more of a momentary event than a lifetime investment in knowing, loving, and obeying the truth of the gospel of Christ. None of it had really become part of him. To that extent, while his Bible study was not wholly a waste of time, its benefits were almost exclusively short term.

The same would probably be true of many Christians. I have often found that to be the case whenever I have used 'The Ephesians Test.'

It only takes a moment or two to take it. But doing so can be the catalyst for a lifetime of better Bible study, both personally and in groups. It is a good test to administer in a group Bible study (especially if you are its leader!)—no one need divulge their answer to the key question; but it has the potential to transform the group's Bible study.

A question

There are so many Bible translations and editions. I personally use *The English Standard Version*[1] of the Bible. I love it and I recommend it. Over the years I seem to have amassed multiple copies: a Study Bible, a Large Print Bible, a Compact Bible, a Wide Margin

---

[1] Published by Crossway Bibles, Wheaton, Illinois, USA.

Bible, A Reference Bible, a Pew Bible, and a Classic Thinline Bible, a Minister's Bible, and yes, I also have a Red Letter Version (although I dislike the idea that Jesus' words should somehow be distinguished in this way. Plus, publishers should know that red letters are more difficult to read as one's eyesight gets poorer!). And then I have other translations as well. The Geneva Bible (I am privileged to have been given a copy published in 1610!); The Authorised (King James) Version, The American Revised Version, The New American Standard Version, The New King James Version, J. N. Darby's Translation, Moffatt's Translation, The New English Bible, The Amplified Bible, The Message, The Living Bible, The New Living Bible, and so on.

In addition, at one time I used to receive a Bible Catalogue every few months which offered for sale an even longer list of Bibles I don't have. The Orthodox Study Bible, The Archaeology Study Bible, The Power of a Praying Woman Bible, The Rainbow Bible, Bibles for children, teens, girls, fellows, youth, sportsmen, soldiers, etc.

Yet, despite all these translations in all the variety of packaging in which they come, it seems that Christians read and understand their Bibles less today than their forefathers did.

Are you one of them?

In some countries the Bible is a banned book. Government agents hunt Bibles down and confiscate them. Imagine for a moment that this happened to your favourite Bible—and in order to prosecute you your Bible was handed over to a CSI Unit ('Crime Scene Investigation')—the kind of law enforcement unit you have probably seen on TV— *Would there be enough recent fingerprint and DNA evidence on your Bible to bring charges against you of being a Christian?*

And would there be enough evidence of a transformed life to secure a conviction against you?

7

Does It Help to Know Some Latin?

or

Christian Baptism

As we entered the university chapel where I was to preach I noticed a large baptismal font. From a distance I thought I could make out the two words which were engraved around it. I did not pause to look at them, but thought 'My guess is those words are ..., but I must come back later and look.' Sure enough, when the service concluded, and I made my way back, my guess had been correct. Two Latin words were inscribed around the font.

If (1) you knew that I was in the chapel of a Lutheran university and (2) you also knew a little about the life of Martin Luther, you would probably have been able to guess what those words were. And even if you knew no Latin you would be able to make an educated guess at how to translate them.

The words were: *Baptizatus sum.*

Translated they mean 'I am a baptized man!'

Martin Luther used to say this whenever he felt himself under pressure and tempted. *'Baptizatus sum!'* (If he taught his beloved wife Katie von Bora to do the same, then she would have said *'Baptizata sum!'*—'I am a baptized woman!').

What was Luther doing? He was saying to himself, 'I need to

remember who I am as a Christian. My baptism tells me that. So, Martin Luther, remember who you are in Christ!'

I sometimes wonder if only a minority of Christians give much thought to the *ongoing* significance of their baptism. And it is doubtful whether many of us under pressure instinctively cry out *'Baptizatus sum!'*

Is baptism so important?

Is baptism all that important? We are not concerned here to rake over the coals of the long-standing controversies that surround baptism. Other books do that.[1] If you find yourself reading and saying 'Yes, but what about …?' you should resist that urge. For here you need to ask a question about your own view of baptism, not that of other Christians. That question is: Whatever view of baptism I hold—*what impact has it had and what difference has it made in my daily life?* Has it played any role in my life in the past week, or month, or even the last year? Have I thought much about it? If not, then whatever may or may not be wrong about others' view of baptism, *there is something wrong with mine!*

Sadly, we are often in danger of making one of two mistakes when we think and talk about baptism.

(1) We may make too much of the 'moment' of baptism and too little of its long-term significance for the rest of our Christian life.

This happens when we think the really, perhaps the only, important thing about baptism is the moment it was administered. Sadly, in churches where infants are baptized, parents sometimes make much of having their son or daughter baptized but then seem to feel that it is 'over and done with.' 'We have had him baptized' is a more

---

[1] For readers interested in exploring one of the chief controversies, the question of who should be baptized—an account of three contrasting views will be found in David F. Wright, ed, *Baptism—Three Views* (Downers Grove, IL: IVP, 2009). The view represented are Credobaptism, Paedobaptism, and Dual Practice.

important consideration than 'What are the implications for us and for our children that they are now baptized?'

On the other hand, someone baptized as a convert may think of their baptism as a great experience in which they confessed Christ, but see it only as a sign of something they did at a specific moment in the past. The net effect is that it has little or no practical function in their ongoing life.

(2) But it is also possible to make too little of its importance and too much of disagreements about it.

We certainly do not believe that the water of baptism has any magical or mystical power. There is nothing special about the water that is used—in most Western countries it will come out of a tap. Using water from the River Jordan has no more power than water from the Mississippi or the Thames. No source of water gives it the power to regenerate us or to 'infuse grace' into us.

Then, again, we may make too much of certain aspects of the water—in debating (a) the amount of water used; (b) the number of times it is used—once, or three times; and (c) whether or not infants of believers should be baptized. In the process we can all too easily divert our focus from the more personal question: What practical function does baptism have in my daily Christian living? The melancholy truth is that it is possible to be convinced you are on the 'right' side of all three of these issues, and yet not really grasp what your baptism was for.

By contrast, the New Testament teaching does not directly discuss these matters; instead it focuses on the question: Is your baptism a functional reality in your life?

Here is one interesting way to think about this that I find instructive. The New Testament contains thirteen letters which begin 'Paul …' Four of them were written to individuals (Philemon, 1 and 2 Timothy, and Titus). Out of the nine letters written to seven different churches, Paul makes specific reference to baptism in no less than five (Romans, 1 Corinthians, Galatians, Ephesians, and Colossians). In addition, Acts records baptisms taking place in one of the other churches (Philippi—Acts 16:25-34). Clearly baptism is important.

Here are some things Paul said. Please note that a quiz follows immediately after you have read them!

> What shall we say then? Are we to continue in sin that grace may abound? By no means! How can we who died to sin still live in it? Do you not know that all of us who have been baptized into Christ Jesus were baptized into his death? We were buried therefore with him by baptism into death, in order that, just as Christ was raised from the dead by the glory of the Father, we too might walk in newness of life. (Rom. 6:1-4)

> For as many of you as were baptized into Christ have put on Christ. (Gal. 3:27)

> In him [Christ] also you were circumcised with a circumcision made without hands, by putting off the body of the flesh, by the circumcision of Christ, having been buried with him in baptism, in which you were also raised with him through faith in the powerful working of God, who raised him from the dead. And you, who were dead in your trespasses and the uncircumcision of your flesh, God made alive together with him, having forgiven us all our trespasses, by cancelling the record of debt that stood against us with its legal demands. This he set aside, nailing it to the cross. He disarmed the rulers and authorities and put them to open shame, by triumphing over them in him. (Col. 2:11-15)

Question: In the letters (or more likely emails) I write to fellow-Christians, to encourage them, how often do I mention baptism?—Mark your answer on the scale below:

50%+   40%+   30%+   20%+   10%+   1%+   0%

What do you think is likely to be the most common answer? I have my own suspicions, don't you?

Granted this is perhaps not a fair test (there would be few authors in Christian history who would do well in it!), the question still functions as a catalyst to cause us to think more seriously about the significance of our baptism.

So, having established its practical importance it will help us a great deal if we can understand:

(1) What baptism is; and (2) What baptism means.

1. *What baptism is*

Baptism is essentially a naming ceremony. In churches where the infant children of believers are baptized this is expressed when the parents are asked 'What is the name of your child?' Or in the ancient traditional services for the baptism of converts, 'What is your name?' Then, as the person is baptized the minister or celebrant will say: 'A. B., I baptize you *in the name of the Father, and of the Son, and of the Holy Spirit.*'

I once had a very delightful and highly intelligent and able doctoral student from Asia. His name was 'Timothy.' One day I had the following conversation with him:

'Timothy, what is your *real* name?'

I noted a moment ago that he had a very sharp mind. He smiled. It was a little smile (although behind it I am sure he knew he was about to teach his professor a theological lesson—which I enjoyed!).

'My real name is "Timothy".'

I smiled in return, thinking—it is impossible that his parents named him 'Timothy'—'Timothy' is NOT an Asian name!

'Come on,' I said, 'What name did your parents give you?'

He replied with a name that was very obviously Asian and not Western. It was definitely *not* 'Timothy'! But then, perhaps noting the beginnings of a triumphant smile appearing on my face, he added, 'But my REAL name is "Timothy". *That is the name I was given when I was baptized.*'

What a great lesson to be taught by a student! He understood the meaning of baptism. He was Asian and he retained his family name. But he no longer thought of himself as he was by birth and nature, but as a person who understood himself in the light of the gospel and the new identity in Christ that baptism proclaims to us throughout our whole life. It tells us who we are 'in Christ' and summons us to live it out day by day. Timothy really understood baptism. So baptism is not just a neat thing to do. It carries lifelong significance.

Think of Jesus' statement when he inaugurated Christian baptism after his resurrection and before he ascended to heaven:

> And Jesus came and said to them, 'All authority in heaven and on earth has been given to me. Go therefore and make disciples of all nations, baptizing them in the name of the Father and of the Son and of the Holy Spirit, teaching them to observe all that I have commanded you. And behold, I am with you always, to the end of the age.' (Matt. 28:18-20)

For the first time in human history, the Lord Jesus revealed how the full name of God should be pronounced. He is no longer to be known as *Yahweh* (i.e. 'Lord'), but as Father, Son, and Holy Spirit. This is the name into which we are baptized.

Jesus' words help us to understand that baptism as such does not change anything *within us*—any more than being given a name does. But, like being given a name, baptism makes a lifelong impact *on us*.

If someone asks me 'Who are you?' I answer in terms of my name. I cannot think about myself, or about my identity, without knowing that I am Sinclair Buchanan Ferguson. When my parents thus named me they no more changed my heart than the water of baptism can.

Yet from another point of view something did happen to me. A name was written into my life so that I cannot really think about myself, or about who I am, apart from that name. I could hate that name and want to repudiate it (I don't!). But I certainly do not and cannot think about myself as 'Angus Ferguson' (apparently my parents' second choice). I am not 'Angus,' I am Sinclair! If I were to suffer temporary amnesia and be asked 'Who are you?' forgetting my name would have serious repercussions for me.

Something similar is true of baptism. It is a naming ceremony. We are baptized into the Name! Again we should insist that we are not changed within by baptism. But at the same time baptism summons us to live the whole of our lives in relation to the Name that has been written on us in water. Of course, I could repudiate the name I was given. Some do, as we shall see.

What baptism means

But there is more to baptism than the naming ceremony. For we are baptized '*into*' the Name. Did a preposition ever hold so much meaning? But what is the meaning?

Baptism is, of course, a washing ritual. But more fundamentally the New Testament relates baptism to the idea that the Christian is united to Jesus Christ, or is 'in Christ.'

Union with Christ is one of the most frequent and central ideas in the New Testament. It is particularly prominent in Paul's letters (he speaks of Christians as being 'in Christ/him' over 150 times). On one occasion, when he seems almost embarrassed by the number of references he is making to himself, he refers to himself by saying 'I know *a man in Christ* …' (2 Cor. 12:2). Paul was simply building on the teaching of Jesus ('I am the Vine, you are the branches … abide in me and I in you …,' John 15:1ff.); and his teaching is shared with other writers in the New Testament.

To be 'in Christ' means that through the work of the Holy Spirit we have come to believe not only 'on' Christ but 'into' Christ. The result is a vital union with him in which everything he has done for us is shared with us. All the resources that are in Christ become ours.

Paul relates this to baptism in the tightly-packed statement in Colossians 2:11-15 already cited. It is worth quoting again:

> In him also you were circumcised with a circumcision made without hands, by putting off the body of the flesh, by the circumcision of Christ, having been buried with him in baptism, in which you were also raised with him through faith in the powerful working of God, who raised him from the dead. And you, who were dead in your trespasses and the uncircumcision of your flesh, God made alive together with him, having forgiven us all our trespasses, by cancelling the record of debt that stood against us with its legal demands. This he set aside, nailing it to the cross. He disarmed the rulers and authorities and put them to open shame, by triumphing over them in him.

This is a very dense paragraph, isn't it? What do all these phrases mean?

For the moment we need look only at the big picture. The easiest way to do this is to think of the whole statement as having two parts. And it probably helps to look at the second part first, because it really serves as the foundation.

Part Two: Colossians 2:13-15

Here Paul is explaining the heart of the gospel to the Colossians.

By his death on the cross, Christ bore our sins and cancelled our debt; all the demands of the law that we should die because of our sins have been fully met by him (verses 14 15)

Having discharged all our debts by his death, Christ rose again—a clear indication that he had satisfied the debt he assumed for our sins.

All this took place before we were born.

In Christ God has wiped our slate clean; and in the here-and-now he has also raised us up from our spiritual death in sin, and brought us into his family (even although we are not circumcised children of Abraham, verse 13).

Part One: Colossians 2:11-12.

This is the more dense part. But the big picture is this. Paul is linking together three things:

- Circumcision (from the Old Testament)

- The death and resurrection of Christ (from the Gospel narrative)

- Baptism (in our experience)

Circumcision was the physical cutting off of the foreskin of eight-day-old boys which Abraham was commanded to inaugurate for his descendants as a sign of God's covenant with him and his seed (Gen. 17:9-14). That covenant included the promise that in his seed all the nations of the world would be blessed (Gen. 12:1-3).

Paul believed that seed was, ultimately, the Lord Jesus (Gal. 3:16).

Jesus himself was circumcised as an eight-day old boy (Luke 2:21). But that was not his real circumcision. It was a physical sign of his real circumcision—which took place when he was (as the prophet Isaiah foresaw) 'cut off out of the land of the living, stricken for the transgression of my people' (Isa. 53:8).

Jesus' real circumcision took place not on his eighth day, but on his crucifixion day.

But Jesus was also baptized, when he was about thirty years old (Luke 3:21-23).[1] It is even clearer in connection with his baptism that it signified another and greater baptism. For later in the Gospel narrative, our Lord said:

---

[1] Jesus' baptism was also a 'naming ceremony' for him. God spoke from heaven in words deliberately reminiscent of Old Testament prophecies about the one who would come. He was 'named' or identified by God as his beloved Son, as the long-promised King, and as the Suffering Servant (Psa. 2:7; Isa. 42:1).

I have a baptism to be baptized with, and how great is my distress until it is accomplished! (Luke 12:50).

He was clearly speaking about his crucifixion—not the baptism in water in the River Jordan at the age of thirty, but the baptism in blood on Mount Calvary at the age of thirty-three. That was his real baptism.

Thus, the meaning of circumcision, the circumcision of every male seed of Abraham—and especially of Jesus' own circumcision— and the meaning of every baptism—and especially of Jesus' own baptism—point in the same direction and to the same event: *the death of Christ for our sins and his resurrection for our justification and new life.* Circumcision pointed forwards while baptism points backwards to Jesus Christ.

When Paul speaks about the meaning of circumcision in Romans 4:11-12 he explains that it was a sign and seal of the righteousness of God that Abraham received by faith.

It is significant—and important to notice—that circumcision was not a sign and seal of the faith itself, but of the good news of grace to which Abraham's faith responded. In other words, the sign was not a sign of Abraham's response, but of God's covenant with him and his promise of justification and salvation.

The same is true of baptism. It is not a sign pointing to me, but to Christ; not to my faith, but to Christ's cross, his death for sin, his burial of the old life, his resurrection power—and it summons me, like a visual gospel sermon, to respond in repentance and faith.

In fact, this is how all of God's signs function—from the rainbow in the sky in the covenant with Noah to the bread and the wine at the new covenant Supper. They do not point to our response to God's grace but to Christ himself. They are not badges of what we have done, but of what he has done. In simple terms, when I see the signs I do not think about myself but about Christ. In that sense it would be appropriate to sing at baptism words we usually associate with heaven:

> The bride eyes not her garment,
> But her dear bridegroom's face;
> I will not gaze at glory,
> But on my King of grace;
> Not at the crown He giveth,
> But on His piercèd hand:
> The Lamb is all the glory
> Of Immanuel's land.[1]

The sign of baptism proclaims the gospel to us; it points us to Christ and all that faith receives from him. The proclamation of the gospel does not say, 'Look at what is happening within you, and you will be saved.' No, it tells us to look away from ourselves, to have faith in Christ alone, and we will be saved. It proclaims: 'In Christ every spiritual blessing is to be found—look to him, not to yourself.' So baptism is a sign of Christ and his work and all it may mean for us, as we respond in faith; it is not a sign of our faith.

It can be quite difficult for some Christians to 'see' this. In a sense 'seeing the picture' in baptism can be like looking at an optical illusion. Think of the optical illusion which viewed one way looks like an old hag, while viewed differently turns out to be a beautiful young woman. I have met people who have told me they have never seen the young woman. It is difficult to convince them that she is 'there.' In the same way, if we have always thought about baptism as 'a sign of my faith,' it may be difficult, emotionally and psychologically to 'let go' of that and to look at the picture from a more biblical angle.

But once we are able to see our baptism through biblically-crafted lenses, we will begin to see that it turns out to be far more relevant to faith *today* than our former view was. We begin to understand that it was a once-for-all-time, life-long sign of the endless riches that are

---

[1] From the hymn 'The sands of time are sinking', composed by Anne Ross Cousin (1824–1906) and based on the words of Samuel Rutherford (c.1600–1661).

ours in Christ. It tells us that our whole Christian life involves leaving behind the old life and receiving every spiritual blessing in and from Christ. It points me to him, not to myself. And so it is not the event of a moment, but the sign under which my whole life is lived 'in Christ.' In Paul's language in Romans 6:1-14, baptism tells me I am someone *who has died to sin and been raised into newness of life*, and summons me to live as a forgiven sinner released from the dominion of sin in the transforming power of Christ's resurrection life.

Think about what that means. It means that, as a believer, remembering that I have been baptized, I realize that my old life has been buried in Christ's tomb. I have no right to return to it. That would be to wish that Christ had remained dead rather than risen in power into newness of life.

Recently, in the wave of 'the New Atheism' that has emerged in the Western world, numbers of people have been demanding a Baptism Renunciation Certificate. They want to repudiate the baptism they received in early life (or in some instances later on)—and want to do so *officially* as it were—to become 'unbaptized.'

Some church members find this appalling. But the truth is people have been repudiating their baptism since the time of the New Testament. The really sad thing is that many of them have remained 'members' of churches. In some ways one wonders if Christ would prefer to have Baptism Renunciation Certificates printed. After all, he sent a letter to the church at Laodicaea with these words:

> Would that you were either cold or hot. So, because you are lukewarm, and neither hot nor cold, I will spit you out of my mouth.
>
> (Rev. 3:15, 16)

And Hebrews 6:4-6 includes these words that might well be appropriate for a Baptism Renunciation Certificate:

> For it is impossible to restore again to repentance those who have once been enlightened, who have tasted the heavenly gift, and have shared in the Holy Spirit, and have tasted the goodness of the word

of God and the powers of the age to come, if they then fall away, since they are crucifying once again the Son of God to their own harm and holding him up to contempt.

But a Baptism Renunciation Certificate cannot reverse the *fact* that we have been baptized. Like rejecting the family name it could never erase the fact that *this is the family we have spurned and rejected.* All it could do would be to say (in Milton's words):

> I reject all these privileges.
> 'Better to reign in hell than serve in heaven.'

But it is unlikely that many who have read thus far will have repudiated baptism.

For us the question is a different one, but it is a very serious one:

Have I entered into all the privileges of my baptism, and am I living in the light of them on a daily basis?

Am I responding faithfully and consistently to all that baptism proclaims to me can be mine through faith-union with Jesus Christ?

The older writers used a quaint expression in this connection. They spoke about 'improving baptism'![1] They simply meant living a baptized life, and being able to say that your baptism means more to you now than it has ever done.

Do you ever say (in any language):

> 'I am a baptized person!' *Baptizatus sum!*

---

[1] See the Appendix to this chapter.

APPENDIX

Since our baptism is a sign of the gospel, and calls us to live Christ-centred, gospel-style lives, it is a constant reminder to us of both our privileges and our obligations. As we think about it day by day, we more and more come to appreciate what it means to be a Christian. When we are discouraged (like Luther) we realize that it points us to the new identity believers have in Christ. If there is any danger of us becoming proud, it reminds us that in ourselves we are sinful—only in Christ are we made new. And it challenges us to live a baptized life—so that someone following us around for a few days might begin to see the difference it makes that we are baptized Christians.

This was something our forefathers well understood and explained. Below is an excerpt from the Larger Catechism, composed at the Westminster Assembly and approved for use in the Church in Scotland in 1648. While the language in places may seem a little quaint, the teaching itself is biblical and helpful.

Q. 167. *How is our baptism to be improved by us?*

A. The needful but much neglected duty of improving our baptism, is to be performed by us all our life long, especially in the time of temptation, and when we are present at the administration of it to others;[1] by serious and thankful consideration of the nature of

---

[1] Colossians 2:11, 12. In him also you were circumcised with a circumcision made without hands, by putting off the body of the flesh, by the circumcision of Christ, having been buried with him in baptism, in which you were also raised with him through faith in the powerful working of God, who raised him from the dead.

Romans 6:4, 6, 11. We were buried therefore with him by baptism into death, in order that, just as Christ was raised from the dead by the glory of the Father, we too might walk in newness of life. … We know that our old self was crucified with him in order that the body of sin might be brought to nothing, so that we would

it, and of the ends for which Christ instituted it, the privileges and benefits conferred and sealed thereby, and our solemn vow made therein;[1] by being humbled for our sinful defilement, our falling short of, and walking contrary to, the grace of baptism, and our engagements;[2] by growing up to assurance of pardon of sin, and of all other blessings sealed to us in that sacrament;[3] by drawing strength from the death and resurrection of Christ, into whom we are baptized, for the mortifying of sin, and quickening of grace;[4]

---

no longer be enslaved to sin. … So you also must consider yourselves dead to sin and alive to God in Christ Jesus.

[1] Romans 6:3-5. Do you not know that all of us who have been baptized into Christ Jesus were baptized into his death? We were buried therefore with him by baptism into death, in order that, just as Christ was raised from the dead by the glory of the Father, we too might walk in newness of life. For if we have been united with him in a death like his, we shall certainly be united with him in a resurrection like his.

[2] 1 Corinthians 1:11-13. For it has been reported to me by Chloe's people that there is quarrelling among you, my brothers. What I mean is that each one of you says,'"I follow Paul,' or 'I follow Apollos,' or 'I follow Cephas,' or 'I follow Christ.' Is Christ divided? Was Paul crucified for you? Or were you baptized in the name of Paul?

Romans 6:2, 3. Or do you not know that the saints will judge the world? And if the world is to be judged by you, are you incompetent to try trivial cases? Do you not know that we are to judge angels? How much more, then, matters pertaining to this life!

[3] Romans 4:11, 12. He received the sign of circumcision as a seal of the righteousness that he had by faith while he was still uncircumcised. The purpose was to make him the father of all who believe without being circumcised, so that righteousness would be counted to them as well, and to make him the father of the circumcised who are not merely circumcised but who also walk in the footsteps of the faith that our father Abraham had before he was circumcised.

1 Peter 3:21. Baptism, which corresponds to this, now saves you, not as a removal of dirt from the body but as an appeal to God for a good conscience, through the resurrection of Jesus Christ.

[4] Romans 6:3-5. Do you not know that all of us who have been baptized into Christ Jesus were baptized into his death? We were buried therefore with him by baptism into death, in order that, just as Christ was raised from the dead by the glory of the Father, we too might walk in newness of life. For if we have been united with him in a death like his, we shall certainly be united with him in a resurrection like his.

and by endeavouring to live by faith,[1] to have our conversation in holiness and righteousness,[2] as those that have therein given up their names to Christ;[3] and to walk in brotherly love, as being baptized by the same Spirit into one body.[4]

---

[1] Galatians 3:26,27. For in Christ Jesus you are all sons of God, through faith. For as many of you as were baptized into Christ have put on Christ.

[2] Romans 6:22. But now that you have been set free from sin and have become slaves of God, the fruit you get leads to sanctification and its end, eternal life.

[3] Acts 2:38. And Peter said to them, "Repent and be baptized every one of you in the name of Jesus Christ for the forgiveness of your sins, and you will receive the gift of the Holy Spirit.

[4] 1 Corinthians 12:13, 25. For in one Spirit we were all baptized into one body-Jews or Greeks, slaves or free – and all were made to drink of one Spirit. ... that there may be no division in the body, but that the members may have the same care for one another.

8

'The Christian's Native Air'[1]

or

Prayer

———

Preachers do not find it easy to preach on it, and most Christian authors probably find it difficult to write about it. Understandably so.

But what is 'it'? *Prayer.*

When I was a young man the editor of a well known publishing house asked me if I would write a book on prayer. I was flattered—both to be asked to write for this particular publisher, but also to be asked to write on prayer, surely a supremely important topic. But I was also hesitant. And so I responded: 'I feel sure there are others who would do a much better job.' The editor quietly asked me who I thought might do it. I mentioned a very well-known and highly respected Christian leader and author. The editor smiled and told me he had asked him already; but the respected author had declined. Was there someone else I might have in mind? I mentioned another name—same response. And another—same response. At least I now knew that I was in good company!

That said, anyone writing a book on believing and belonging must overcome his reluctance in order to write a chapter on prayer.

———

[1] From the hymn 'Prayer is the soul's sincere desire' by James Montgomery (1771–1854).

It must be done, because prayer is one of the central components of life in the fellowship of the church. Luke makes this clear in several of his snapshot pictures of the first Christian church in the early chapters of the Acts of the Apostles.[1]

There are many passages in Scripture to which we could turn to provide a solid foundation for thinking together about prayer. But perhaps a good place to start is the simple statement of Psalm 109:4b:

> I give myself to prayer.

Some of the Psalms carry introductions that tell us about the immediate context which inspired them. Psalm 51 is perhaps the most famous example: 'A Psalm of David. When Nathan the prophet went to him after he had gone in to Bathsheba.' We are meant to read this Psalm in tandem with 2 Samuel 11–12 and interpret it in the light of David's sin. Then, on that basis, we can make David's words our own, applying them to our sinfulness. Yet interestingly, even a Psalm like this, which gives us definite indications about its origin, makes no mention of the details of David's sin. It is not so specific that we cannot apply it to a wide variety of individual experiences. So with many Psalms. On the other hand, there are Psalms which give no hint of the specific context in which they were first written.

Psalm 109 is one such. Nevertheless it is clear that the psalmist was going through difficult days. He was being maligned and haunted by others—probably by one person in particular. Early in the psalm he makes this striking statement:

> In return for my love they accuse me,
>> but I give myself to prayer. (Psa. 109:4)

His enemies *speak against* him; he *speaks to* God.

In my very first week at university I learned something about the original Hebrew of this verse (although not in a Hebrew class!).

---

[1] See Acts 1:12-14, 24; 2:42; 3:1; 4:23-31; 6:4-6.

I owned little more than a shelf of Christian literature. On it was a daily devotional book a friend had given me. Compiled by Mrs Charles E. Cowman it was entitled *Streams in the Desert*. The entry I read for September 29 indicated that the Hebrew text of Psalm 109:4b is simply, 'I prayer' or 'I am prayer'—as the footnote reference in the ESV indicates.

The words leapt off the page. They seemed like a jewel against the dark backcloth of the psalmist's experience. He prayed, yes. But this language suggested something deeper, something intrinsic in him. I was reminded of the hymn by James Montgomery (1771–1854):

> Prayer is the Christian's vital breath,
> > The Christian's native air.

Christians do not simply say prayers; in a sense they become their prayers. Our 'prayer life' as people sometimes call the discipline of specific prayer, and the vital gatherings for prayer which ought to mark every church, are really an expression of our whole life. For prayer is the way in which we express to God our inmost being and our sense of need to him. We do not merely 'say a prayer'; our life becomes a *living prayer*. The musician and song-writer Ron Block expressed this when he composed 'A Living Prayer':

> In Your love I find release,
> > A haven from my unbelief.
> Take my life, and let me be
> > A living prayer, my God, to Thee.[1]

What does it mean to be a 'living prayer' like this? And what are its implications?

---

[1] 'A Living Prayer' has been recorded by Alison Krauss and Union Station on *Lonely Runs Both Ways* (Decca, 2008), and also by the English tenor Alfie Boe on his *You'll Never Walk Alone—The Collection* (EMI, 2011). Ron Block is a member of Union Station; Alfie Boe is probably most widely known for playing the part of Jean Valjean in the musical *Les Misérables*.

Most obviously—and yet perhaps not so obvious?—is that while we *praise God* because he is great and glorious, we *pray to him* because we are weak and in need.

Weakness and need

In fact the whole of Psalm 109 is punctuated by expressions of great weakness and need. When we meet David here he is *in extremis:*

> For I am poor and needy
> and my heart is stricken within me.
> I am gone like a shadow at evening;
> I am shaken off like a locust. (Verses 22, 23)

He is surrounded by enemies who hate him and slander him unjustly. Fasting seems to have done nothing but weaken him more:

> My knees are weak through fasting;
> my body has become gaunt, with no fat. (Verse 24)

Despite his religious exercises he remains—

> an object of scorn to my accusers;
> when they see me, they wag their heads.

And all this is true even while he appeals to the covenant character and promises of God:

> Deal on my behalf for your name's sake;
> because your steadfast love is good,
> deliver me. (Verse 21)

Dr O. Hallesby was surely right when he wrote in his classic study of prayer that 'Prayer has been ordained only for the helpless … Only he who is helpless can truly pray.'[1] Intercession is our telling God: 'We cannot, only you can.' In this sense prayer is not something we do for God. Nor did David think of prayer as 'the way God

---

[1] O. Hallesby, *Prayer*, trans. by C. J. Carlsen (London: Inter-Varsity Press, 1948), p. 13.

speaks to me' (since he does that through his word).[1] No, prayer like this is nothing other than an expression of our need for God and of the faith in which we both express those needs and entrust ourselves to him.

Paul highlights this in his profoundly moving words in Romans 8:26, 27:

> Likewise the Spirit helps us in our weakness. For we do not know what to pray for as we ought, but the Spirit himself intercedes for us with groanings too deep for words. And he who searches hearts knows what is the mind of the Spirit, because the Spirit intercedes for the saints according to the will of God.

So prayer is already an expression of our weakness. But what if, as we pour out our weakness in prayer, it is intensified by the fact that we do not even know what to pray for as we ought? This is weakness taken to a different level, weakness wrapped up in further weakness.

In the church family we become conscious of this weakness when a tragedy occurs, or a crisis arises. Should we pray for this, or for that, or for … what? But in truth we always have this weakness.

God neither despises nor demeans us when we kneel down to pray but find that we are scarcely able to tell him what we feel we or others need. Nor does he suggest that the whole exercise is pointless.

---

[1] This, perhaps, is one of the most common statements people make about prayer. But while we do have communion with God while we pray, and in the midst of our praying light may dawn, if that light truly comes from him its source is his written word, now illumined to us by the Holy Spirit. Understand this dynamic—God speaks through his word in Scripture, brings it to mind and illumines our understanding of it by the Spirit—and we may be saved from a good deal of the confusion caused by contemporary forms of mysticism. When in the psalms moments of illumination come, they often begin with the words 'But you …' A little reflection on these passages indicates that what has happened to the psalmist is that the revelation of God's character, the truth of his promises, and the reliability of his sovereign hand in providence have been brought to mind (by the Spirit) and light has dawned. The psalmist does not reconstruct this in terms of an individual revelation that is known exclusively by himself.

In fact, *virtually the reverse is true*. Paul tells us that this helplessness, this weakness, is taken up by the Spirit and translated into coherent, God-pleasing prayer. The result is 'groanings too deep for words' which nevertheless constitute a language known both to the Spirit who intercedes for us and the Father who hears the groans emerging from deep within us.[1] Clearly there is a great mystery here—but then we understand only the outlines of God's ways, which, as Isaiah records, are so much higher than ours (Isa. 55:8)—and, we might add, much deeper too.

The book of Psalms was Jesus' prayer book. He saw his own experience delineated in it in outline form, and its profound relevance to his own life.

Psalm 109:6-8 provides us with an example of this:

> Appoint a wicked man against him;
>   let an accuser stand at his right hand.
> When he is tried, let him come forth guilty;
>   let his prayer be counted as sin!
> May his days be few;
>   may another take his office!

The early church applied these words to Judas Iscariot and to the appointment of an apostle to take his place.[2] Since the book of Psalms was their prayer book and their hymn book, as well as being part of their school text book, we might well wonder whether the apostles had ever heard Jesus sing or recite these words—but only now did it dawn on them that they actually *were* his words. If so, they must have realized that David's experience, while real and personal, served another and greater function—to point to Jesus. Ultimately we might say it is Jesus, not David, who fully experiences

---

[1] Some scholars have understood these 'groanings' as a reference to speaking in tongues (1 Cor. 14:6-19). But 'speaking in tongues' constitutes a language which by definition employs 'words'; Paul is speaking about a reality 'too deep for words' and therefore not in terms of spoken languages.

[2] See Acts 1:20.

what is described in the Psalm. Jesus knew what it was to cry out in a sense of helplessness to God. In the Garden of Gethsemane he 'offered up prayers and supplications with loud cries and tears, to him who was able to save him from death, and he was heard because of his reverence' (Heb. 5:7). Yes, prayer was an expression of help-lessness and of faith for Jesus too.

Our wise forefathers in the faith used to say that our greatest need is not to feel we have any need, and not realizing that Jesus' words are true that 'apart from me you can do nothing' (John 15:5)—not even pray. Especially not pray. We need to learn that lesson now; because when we find ourselves in a time of darkness and crisis it is usually too late to begin to learn it.

But prayer is more than an expression of our need.

A way of life

We do, and should engage in prayer in a regular way. But these specific times of prayer need to grow out of a prayerful life, a grow-ing sense that we live constantly in the presence and before the face of our Heavenly Father. So much is this the case that—as we have noted—James Montgomery, the nineteenth century hymn-writer, could say:

> Prayer is the Christian's vital breath,
>> The Christian's native air.

I was seventeen when I began to read *Streams in the Desert*. That same year I started reading a much more famous book I owned— Brother Lawrence's *The Practice of the Presence of God*.

Lawrence of the Resurrection (1614–91)—his given name was Nicolas Herman—was a lay monk in the Carmelite Priory in sev-enteenth-century Paris. The book is by no means perfect. But the title, and the idea it represented—living the whole of our lives in the presence of God—fascinated and then gripped me. Soon enough I would become familiar with the description John Calvin (1509–64) had earlier given to the same discipline—living *coram Deo*, in the presence and before the face of God.

As Christians we live in a world where the moral and spiritual atmosphere is polluted. But by God's grace we can be constantly breathing in the pure oxygen of another world, living in an atmosphere of prayerful communion with God. Thus we can share every experience with him. The 'line' between us is always open. The apostle John found this to be a reality. He wrote with a sense of wonder that, through the Holy Spirit 'our fellowship is with the Father, and with his Son Jesus Christ' (1 John 1:3). We thus learn, as Paul urges us, to 'pray always' (1 Thess. 5:17), and as our forefathers liked to say, to 'keep short accounts with God.' We know we are known by him; we hide nothing from him; we share everything with him.

In this way a deep vein of truth runs through the principle that was especially enshrined in the order of monks founded by Benedict, *laborare est orare* (to work is to pray). But we must not malform the motto to mean 'work is a substitute for prayer.' No, for work to become prayer we need to pray as we work, to offer all things to the Lord; to grow in the consciousness that we live before his face; to desire in all things to glorify and enjoy him in everything we do. In a word, to practise the presence of God.

This leads to a third emphasis.

Discipline

While it is true that

> Prayer is the Christian's vital breath
> The Christian's native air,

we should not imagine that prayer is always easy. Christians have been given a new heart, to use the biblical metaphor. But sin continues to damage it, the oxygen levels in the atmosphere are low, the air we breathe is polluted, the food we are fed by the world clogs our spiritual arteries. And so, spiritually, just as naturally, we need to take care of our health. That involves a certain discipline.

One of the longest chapters in O. Hallesby's classic study of prayer has the title 'Prayer as Work.'[1] While the motto *laborare est orare,* may be true enough, the reverse is also valid—*orare est laborare*—to pray is to work. It involves discipline, effort, and commitment.

That same week I was reading the words 'I will give myself to prayer,' something else significant happened. I had been a Christian a few years. I was committed to following Christ and to studying my Bible and growing in prayer. But I was inwardly a very shy seventeen-year-old, just beginning university, and far away from home (at least so it seemed). I had been a member of the Scripture Union since I was nine, and wore its little lapel badge on my jacket.[2] As I was going upstairs in my hall of residence one evening, another student passed me. He spotted the badge, pointed at it, and said 'You will find another one of these in room ___' and kept walking downstairs! Very cloak and dagger!

Later that night I knocked on the door, explained the reason for my mysterious visit, and was welcomed in as a young brother in Christ. Soon I was introduced to other Christians in the residence who helped and encouraged me on the way.

The reason I mention all this is because this was the first time in my life I had a bedroom entirely to myself. I had always shared with my brother. Perhaps it was this new-found luxury that meant it was easier for me to enjoy total privacy to read and to pray. In

---

[1] Hallesby *Prayer*, pp. 51-72

[2] Scripture Union began in 1879 as an offshoot of the Children's Special Service Mission, an organization committed to mission to children. Its aim is to encourage and nurture the regular reading of Scripture. Over the years, beginning with a simple card providing a list of daily Bible readings for the year, it has developed a programme of materials to help people of all ages and stages of the Christian life to read and study the Scriptures each day on their own or in families.

any event, some weeks later when my new friend asked me, 'How are you getting on spiritually?' I naively told him that I had never found prayer easier or more enjoyable. His response? 'Enjoy it then; it may not always be like that.' At the time it was a dampener on my spirits! But I have never forgotten his words—probably because they turned out to be true. In many ways the Lord was treating me as one of the lambs of the flock:

> He will tend his flock like a shepherd;
>   he will gather the lambs in his arms;
> he will carry them in his bosom,
>   and gently lead those that are with young. (Isa. 40:11)

Hebrew has several words for a lamb. The one used here is particularly interesting because it refers to newly-born lambs. Derived from this word is the term Jesus used with such tenderness when he raised Jairus' daughter with the words '*talitha cumi*' (Mark 4:41). The masculine equivalent is *talya*, a little boy. That is what I was—and he was carrying me in his arms. That was surely part of the explanation for how easy prayer seemed. I was being 'carried' without realizing he was bearing my weight! But the time comes when good shepherds let the lambs down on the ground because they need to learn to walk. Watching their early efforts at walking, staggering a little to keep steady—that is just how it often is as we grow as Christians. Prayer, then, may not be so easy. It becomes a battle to find time, and to focus our minds, and to consciously seek God's face. Yes, discipline is needed. For prayer is often hard work.

As the wise spiritual guide he was, the author of *Prayer* commented that unless we see prayer as work we may never get round to including it in our schedule as a basic discipline in our lives. It will be treated as an optional extra. When finances get difficult for us the little 'extras' are the first things to go—sadly, when time is at a premium, and we have so many responsibilities, the same may be true of prayer.

We are given a fine example of this principle of prayer as work in the relatively obscure New Testament figure of Epaphras.

Epaphras was a member—perhaps a pastor—in the church at Colossae. Paul describes him in this way:

> Epaphras, who is one of you, a servant of Christ Jesus, greets you, always *struggling on your behalf in his prayers, that you may stand mature and fully assured in all the will of God.*(Col. 4:12)

Paul uses the verb *agōnizomai.* You do not need to know any Greek to be able to guess what it signifies—it is the root of our word 'agonize.' Epaphras, with all his clear vision of what the Colossians needed, discovered that praying for these people he loved was hard work indeed; it involved discipline and even pain.

I had an elderly friend from Northern Ireland whose life was an echo of Epaphras. He was a banker by profession, had what Celts would call a 'pawky' sense of humour, and was a lifelong bachelor (whenever we asked him why he had never married his answer was always the same: 'Well, the desirable was never possible, and the possible was never desirable!'). He taught a Bible class for high school boys, and had declined any further professional advance in order to continue to do it. Many of his 'boys' distinguished themselves in various professions; an unusual number of them became ministers. He followed their ministries with interest and ongoing encouragement. He prayed for them. When he died the police had to be called to break into his house. They found him on his knees, the prayer list of his 'boys' open beside him.

A congregation of men and women like that, like Epaphras—that would be a church worth belonging to, wouldn't it?

But would it? Wouldn't that imply that *we too* were willing to share in the great struggle for others that is involved in learning to pray?

We read about people like Epaphras who stand out for their spiritual maturity. But most of us feel we live in shallower waters. What we need is not so much advanced training but help to get started, or just to keep going. Is there something that can help us 'ordinary' church members?

The Lord provides us with two basic helps; first, a prayer to help us get us started, and then a fellowship to help us keep going.

A prayer to get us started

This is where our Lord's well-known teaching comes into its own to help us. In earlier centuries, along with the Ten Commandments and the Apostles' Creed, every Christian was expected to memorize it and to use it. Even today it is the one part of the New Testament people tend to know by heart. Most of us are familiar with it in the wording Matthew records in The Sermon on the Mount:

Pray then like this:

> Our Father in heaven,
> hallowed be your name.
> Your kingdom come,
> your will be done,
>   on earth as it is in heaven.
> Give us this day our daily bread,
> and forgive us our debts,
>   as we also have forgiven our debtors.
> And lead us not into temptation,
> but deliver us from evil. (Matt. 6:9-13)

Luke tells us Jesus also taught the same prayer when a disciple, hearing him pray, asked, 'Lord, teach us to pray—just as John taught his disciples' (Luke 11:1). Our Lord knew that most people learn to pray not by being given a series of principles, or by reading a chapter on prayer in a systematic theology text book (important though these may be), but by example and illustration. This particular disciple already had a desire kindled in his heart by listening to how Jesus prayed (did he say to himself 'I wish I could pray like that'?). Now Jesus gave him words as well. But these were not only words. Presumably the Saviour did not merely intend him to say these words by rote—it takes less than a minute to repeat them quite slowly. No, it looks as though Jesus was giving the man a start, an outline, a simple pattern that would help him. The Lord's Prayer is a summary prayer. It is as though Jesus were saying 'Here, memorize these words, and they will never fail to get you started.'

In my grandmother's day peppermints were popular. What impressed me as a child was how long 'really old' people could suck a single peppermint. They could make it last … and *last* … and LAST! I, by contrast, was a peppermint *crusher*. One never lasted long. Sometimes people 'crush' the Lord's Prayer: 'saying my prayers' means a hurried repetition of the words—thirty seconds and it is done and dusted for another day. But that is to misuse it. No. We are meant to linger on each phrase, and to use it as a catalyst for our own words. As we do so we will discover that in a truly remarkable way these few words provide us with a starting place for everything we need to express when we seek God's face in prayer:

Our Father in heaven—we have the privilege of coming into his presence

Our Father in heaven—we are conscious that we belong to his family

Hallowed be your Name—we want to see him reverenced and worshipped

Your kingdom come—we are concerned to see his reign in our lives and in the world

Your will be done—we want to acknowledge that he is Lord and yield to his will, word and providence

On earth as it is in heaven—we know that in heaven he is worshiped perfectly and we want to as well

Give us this day our daily bread—we depend on him for everything and ask him to sustain us daily

Forgive us our debts—we confess that we have sinned, and we ask for pardon

As we forgive our debtors—we know that the sign of a forgiven sinner is forgiving other sinners

And lead us not into temptation—we acknowledge how frail we are and how easily we yield

But deliver us from evil—we seek his grace to protect and free us from spiritual enemies and danger:

Each of these petitions will then naturally become a stimulus and launching pad for our own prayers of adoration, confession, thanksgiving, supplication and intercession. As we grow in spiritual experience we should find ourselves growing in the way we use this prayer. Yes, it will often still be a battle—a fight for time, or with wandering thoughts, or because of crushing burdens. But we will learn how to pray—and we will discover that we never come to the end of using the Lord's Prayer.

But there is another important help:

A fellowship to help us keep going

We pray '*our* Father,' not '*my* Father' because we come to him in Christ not as isolated individuals but as members of his family.

The only person in the New Testament who actually *addresses* God as his Father using the first person singular pronoun is the Lord Jesus himself.[1] The Lord's Prayer teaches us to use the first person

---

[1] Jesus frequently refers to God as 'my Father.' Only once does he address him as 'my God'—in his cry of dereliction on the cross. Paul also uses the expression 'my God' when he refers to him supplying the needs of his people (Phil. 4:19). There is a connection between these two uses: God supplies us in our time of deepest need through turning his face away from his Son when he entered into his time of deepest sense of need in dying for us on the cross.

plural when we speak to God—*our* Father. This in turn creates in us a deep-seated instinct that we come to him as members of his family, not as isolated individuals.

As we will also notice in connection with evangelism, prayer is an area in which Christians have probably been encouraged to think too individualistically. We therefore tend to lose sight of the corporate dimension of prayer.

By contrast Luke's description of the first church in Jerusalem emphasizes that prayer was a *corporate* activity. Doubtless its members prayed individually; but what is emphasized is that *they met together to pray*. As Luke shows us a kind of video-recording of those early days he presses the pause button every so often to make his point:

> All these with one accord were devoting themselves to prayer, together with the women and Mary the mother of Jesus, and his brothers. (Acts 1:14)

> And they devoted themselves to the apostles' teaching and the fellowship, to the breaking of bread and the prayers. (2:42)

> Now Peter and John were going up to the temple at the hour of prayer, the ninth hour. (3:1)

> And when they heard it, they lifted their voices together to God and said, 'Sovereign Lord, who made the heaven and the earth and the sea and everything in them, who through the mouth of our father David, your servant, said by the Holy Spirit,
>
>> "Why did the Gentiles rage,
>>   and the peoples plot in vain?
>> The kings of the earth set themselves,
>>   and the rulers were gathered together,
>>   against the Lord and against his Anointed"—
>
> for truly in this city there were gathered together against your holy servant Jesus, whom you anointed, both Herod and Pontius Pilate, along with the Gentiles and the peoples of Israel, to do whatever

your hand and your plan had predestined to take place. And now, Lord, look upon their threats and grant to your servants to continue to speak your word with all boldness, while you stretch out your hand to heal, and signs and wonders are performed through the name of your holy servant Jesus.' And when they had prayed, the place in which they were gathered together was shaken, and they were all filled with the Holy Spirit and continued to speak the word of God with boldness. (4:24-31)

But we will devote ourselves to prayer and to the ministry of the word. (6:4)

Peter was kept in prison, but earnest prayer for him was made to God by the church. (12:5)

It was in this context that the first Christians found so much encouragement to pray. Today we still need that encouragement.

It is possible that in some ways we need even more encouragement to pray. If we are honest we will probably admit that the subject of prayer is often 'the elephant in the room' when our churches come to set their priorities. This is true not only at the individual level ('How are you getting on in prayer these days?' might well seem a step too far, or at least the answers might be very sobering to hear, if our church leaders were to ask the question of us one by one). It seems to be true particularly of churches' corporate gatherings for prayer. They are, in many churches—perhaps even most—among the most poorly attended meetings of all.

One of the first things a guest preacher sometimes receives when he arrives at a church is a worship bulletin of some kind or another. Many of these also include notices about the church calendar for the week. The first thing I have always looked for is not the hymns that will be sung but to see when, if at all, this congregation gathers for prayer. Over the years I have noticed that many churches seem to have no point in their calendar when the congregation comes together to pray. Or, enquiring about prayer gatherings, people will say that they are poorly attended, indeed often the worst attended of all meetings.

Yet in all our churches we say that 'we believe in prayer.'

Perhaps these words are a symptom of the basic problem. We may believe that God hears and answers prayer; but if we 'believe in prayer' our faith is misplaced. We still believe in what *we can do*. We have not yet come to an end of ourselves to see or feel the deep-seated need we have of God, and to see that prayer expresses our weakness not our strength. It is hardly surprising then that we do not gather together as a church to cry to God for his help. Seeing, knowing, and feeling our needs would transform our priorities.

Thoughtful Christians are deeply disturbed by this modern-day phenomenon of apparent indifference to corporate prayer in our churches. They could be forgiven for wondering if the sometimes vast edifices we build and the large congregations that sometimes gather on a Sunday morning have any real substance if, apart from the prayers during the services, the entire project seems to have been built *prayerlessly*. Why the concern? Because prayerlessness is a kind of practical atheism.

Wise church leaders realize that the structure of our lives in the twenty-first century is very different and much more complicated than was true a hundred years ago. They know that there is neither commandment nor example in the New Testament that suggests 'Thou shalt have a mid-week prayer meeting on Wednesday nights.' At the same time, they see how important praying together was for the New Testament church. It may be that a larger central meeting is impractical—for whatever reasons. If so, then ways need to be found to punctuate the week with opportunities for corporate prayer, whether mid-week, or before services, early in the morning, at church Bible studies, or in other small groups. Surely the church that never comes together for prayer loses something. Apart from other considerations there is no better way to get to know both the church and the hearts of your fellow members. But however our church configures itself for prayer, we should follow the pattern. We need to pray *together*.

I remember being deeply impressed by some words of an elder, a banker by profession until his retirement. He told me that on some Wednesday evenings (when the church held its main corporate prayer meeting) 'I had to drag myself to the prayer meeting.' I really admired him for that. He understood that prayer is work. And as—not least through his participation—these gatherings had become such vibrant and spiritually helpful occasions, I was able to say to him, 'Yes; but you usually didn't have to drag yourself home afterwards, did you, such was the blessing we experienced!'

Like my friend the elder, I have often found attendance at prayer meetings a severe discipline, a task one could so easily put off until next week—except for the fact that you well know it will not be any easier to pray then.

Remember what all the manuals that teach effective work practices tell you to do? *Do the difficult things first. Give them priority.* My own experience, for what it is worth, is that disciplined faithful attendance at corporate prayer times can slowly transform them into some of the best and most important meetings you attend. Apart from other considerations, the privilege of hearing the burdens on the hearts of Christian friends is a better way to get to know them than having coffee with them! In no other context in life will you hear the kind of speech that is expressed when believers share their needs and desires with God. The quickest way to get into the heart of a church is to gather with it when it turns to prayer.

Sometimes ministers and preachers day-dream of being able to preach like someone else, perhaps like some great preacher from the past. A Baptist minister might well dream of being able to preach like Charles Haddon Spurgeon (1834–92). But actually in order to preach like him you would need to find his secret. A visitor to the

Metropolitan Tabernacle in London (where he was minister) once asked him what that secret was. 'The secret is in here!' he said as they came to a door in the church building. Spurgeon then opened the door—into a prayer meeting where perhaps twelve hundred people were gathered to pray for the ministry. The church was showing that it was truly apostolic—giving itself 'to prayer and the ministry of the word' (Acts 6:4). How thrilling that must have been! And yet many of those present must have 'dragged themselves' there in their weariness from work. But few of them went home weary of the work!

> Prayer is the soul's sincere desire,
>   Unuttered or expressed;
> The motion of a hidden fire
>   That trembles in the breast.
>
> Prayer is the burden of a sigh,
>   The falling of a tear;
> The upward glancing of an eye,
>   When none but God is near.
>
> Prayer is the simplest form of speech
>   That infant lips can try;
> Prayer the sublimest strains that reach
>   The Majesty on high.
>
> Prayer is the Christian's vital breath,
>   The Christian's native air;
> His watchword at the gates of death;
>   He enters Heav'n with prayer.
>
> Prayer is the contrite sinner's voice,
>   Returning from his ways;
> While angels in their songs rejoice,
>   And cry, 'Behold, he prays!'
>
> The saints in prayer appear as one
>   In word, in deed, and mind;
> While with the Father and the Son
>   Sweet fellowship they find.

Nor prayer is made by man alone,
　The Holy Spirit pleads,
And Jesus, on the eternal throne,
　For sinners intercedes.

O Thou by whom we come to God,
　The Life, the Truth, the Way,
The path of prayer Thyself hast trod;
　Lord, teach us how to pray.

(James Montgomery)

9

The View from the Foot

or

Christian Service

Some small events seem to fix themselves in our memory and grow larger in the way they teach us lifelong lessons.

Years ago I was sitting at a dinner that followed a wedding at which I was a guest. The meal was well underway, guests were talking together, and everything seemed to be going smoothly. Suddenly the banqueting room was momentarily plunged into the shocked silenced that always follows the sound of the crashing of plates. One of the servers, just beside our table, had slipped. Plates were all over the place. The rest of the staff continued as if nothing had happened (presumably that was what they had been trained to do, otherwise the entire proceedings might grind to a halt).

I turned to a long-time friend—a Presbyterian minister as it happens—who was sitting beside me, and thoughtlessly commented '*Somebody* should be helping that poor girl!'

He looked at me (did I detect a slight smile playing on his lips as a word began to form on them?). Quietly he said: 'Well?'—meaning 'Somebody? Do you mean "somebody else, but not me"?'

Duly chastened I rose from my seat and tried to do something to help. In my defence I might say that I did this willingly, and in a good spirit! But sadly, were it not for my friend's gentle finger-pointing, I might have done nothing. After all, 'somebody' usually means 'somebody else.'

Of course the illustration would have been all the more dramatic if I were to climax it by saying: 'And I was the bridegroom whose wedding the banquet was celebrating.'

That was not the case on this occasion. But interestingly John describes two events, one at the beginning and the other at the end of Jesus' public ministry both of which involved potential disasters at celebratory meals.

The first is in John 2:1-11 when Jesus came to the rescue at a wedding feast. The second took place in the Upper Room where Jesus had gathered with the apostles to celebrate a Passover meal, and is described in John 13:1-12. On this occasion he did something in many ways much more remarkable. In John 2 Jesus helped the bridegroom. But in the events that are described in John 13, Jesus was the Bridegroom (Matt. 9:15; John 3:29):

> Now before the Feast of the Passover, when Jesus knew that his hour had come to depart out of this world to the Father, having loved his own who were in the world, he loved them to the end. During supper, when the devil had already put it into the heart of Judas Iscariot, Simon's son, to betray him, Jesus, knowing that the Father had given all things into his hands, and that he had come from God and was going back to God, rose from supper. He laid aside his outer garments, and taking a towel, tied it around his waist. Then he poured water into a basin and began to wash the disciples' feet and to wipe them with the towel that was wrapped around him …
>
> When he had washed their feet and put on his outer garments and resumed his place, he said to them, 'Do you understand what I have done to you? You call me Teacher and Lord, and you are right, for so I am. If I then, your Lord and Teacher, have washed your feet, you also ought to wash one another's feet. For I have given you an example, that you also should do just as I have done to you. Truly, truly, I say to you, a servant is not greater than his

master, nor is a messenger greater than the one who sent him. If
you know these things, blessed are you if you do them.'

(John 13:1-5; 12-17)

These moments must have stunned the apostles. But as John
reflected on what Jesus did and said he realized that he had witnessed an event in two dimensions, as it were. One dimension he
understood that night; the other must have taken time to dawn on
him. When he came to write his Gospel, he wove these two dimensions together as he narrated the event.

At a profound level—which could only have dawned on John
later on—Jesus' action of washing his disciples' feet was a kind of
dramatic parable of the gospel. John even tells us what was going on
in Jesus' mind—just as Paul did in Philippians 2:5-11. In fact there
are illuminating parallels between John's description of Jesus' actions
and Paul's statements. Both reveal what Paul calls 'the mind' of Jesus
Christ (Phil. 2:5) which Christians are also to express.

JOHN	PAUL
Jesus, knowing that the Father had given all things into his hands, and that he had come from God	Being in the form of God
Rose from supper	Did not count equality with God a thing to be grasped
He laid aside his outer garments,	But made himself nothing
And taking a towel, tied it around his waist	Taking the form of a servant
Then he poured water into a basin and began to wash the disciples' feet and to wipe them with the towel that was wrapped around him …	Being found in human form he humbled himself by becoming obedient to the point of death, even death on a cross
When he had washed their feet and put on his outer garments and resumed his place …	Therefore God has highly exalted him and bestowed on him the name that is above every name …

But at another level, in one sense a more mundane level, Jesus was teaching his disciples a basic lesson about their relationship to one another in the family of God:

> If I then, your Lord and Teacher, have washed your feet, you also ought to wash one another's feet. (John 13:14)

The mind of Christ

In the Bible the term 'mind' can express all the different nuances of meaning it has in English.

Sometimes we use it to express the idea of the intellect ('He has a brilliant mind'); at other times we use it to express attitudes ('Do you mind if I do this'—where 'mind' really means attitude rather than intelligence); or affections, desires, dispositions ('Do you have a mind to play golf today?'). We even use it to express caring about, and looking out for someone ('Would you mind my child while I run an errand?'). The precise meaning of 'mind'—like all words—depends on how it is used in a specific context.

When Paul speaks about the mind of Christ he is not thinking about our Lord's intelligence, but about how he thought about himself, his attitude to his own life. When John describes the way Jesus washed his disciples' feet on the evening of his crucifixion he also describes our Lord's mind or attitude both to them and to himself.

Jesus was conscious that he was the Son of God, and that he had come into the world from the glory of God. He knew the Father had put all things under his authority, and that he had both come from God and was returning to him. The prayer of Jesus some time later (recorded in John 17) makes this very clear.

Fully conscious of his own glorious identity, he rose from the table, poured water into a basin, and went to his disciples one by one to wash their feet.

We could guess the context of this simply from what was happening. But we do not need to guess. Luke tells us that in the Upper

Room the disciples were arguing about position (Luke 22:24-27)—and not for the first time (Luke 9:46). With that spirit still lingering in the atmosphere, when they arrived at the Upper Room—which had been prepared for them so that Jesus could have an undisturbed final meal with them on their own—none of them had been willing to do what a household servant normally would have done. Each of them sat at table with unwashed feet rather than show a little humility by kneeling down before his fellow disciples and washing their feet.

What a moment it must have been when Jesus rose from the low table, and it became obvious what he was planning to do. Perhaps only Peter protested out loud in his typically muddle-headed way (John 13:6-9); but everyone in the room must have felt the incongruity of what was happening. *Everyone?* No, there were probably two exceptions. Jesus perfectly understood what he was doing; Judas Iscariot's heart was now too hard to care.

Jesus got up from the place of honour, took off his robe, tied the towel to his waist, and washed and dried the feet of each of the twelve.

Twelve? Is that not a misprint, a miscalculation? Eleven, surely? Surely not Judas?

Yes, Judas too! John's narrative indicates that he was still in the room.[1] What a scene—the Lord of glory kneels at the feet of his betrayer! Truly Jesus 'loved them to the end.' The great Dutch New Testament scholar Herman Ridderbos expressed it beautifully: 'It was love to the last breath and love in its highest intensity.'[2]

Here Jesus reveals the servant's heart, and John describes what is involved in 'the mind of Christ,' and then we learn the basic pattern for a life of service to others.

[1] John 13:21-30 makes this clear.
[2] H. N. Ridderbos, *The Gospel of John, A Theological Commentary* (Dutch ed. in 2 vols, Kampen: J. H. Kok, 1987, 1992; English ed., trans. John Vriend, Grand Rapids: Eerdmans, 1997), p. 452.

1. *Jesus saw what was needed.* 'Somebody' needed to wash the feet of the disciples. Jesus saw the need and did what was needed.

That is not something we can learn to do mechanically. It comes from the heart, not from a formula. It is a style of life, not a system.

Some Christians appear to be specially gifted in this area—they possess an unusual aptitude for problem-solving in relation to others' personal needs, just as other people have an instinctive ability to be 'good with their hands.' Perhaps this is what Paul means by 'helping' (1 Cor. 12:28). But if so, like every other gift its genius involves a willing and humble spirit and hard work—actually using the gift in order to help others.

2. *Jesus was willing to leave the position to which he was entitled* in order to serve others. The 'mind of Christ' also involves 'the will of Christ.' We follow his example of service by doing, not merely by seeing! With him there was no spirit of 'somebody ought to, but not me.'

3. *Jesus was prepared to engage in such a humble task* because he was committed to even greater acts of humility. This is the hallmark of humility. To be prepared to do *A* but not to stoop lower to do *B* means we are still controlled by our pride, and not by the mind of Christ.

What determined the way our Lord thought here? This: since he had come into the world to die for his disciples, washing their feet was a small matter. In other words, this humble act was a little thing by comparison with coming from God in order to be humiliated on the cross for our sins. That, supremely, was the measure of his loving commitment to serve them. Since he was willing to be stripped and humiliated on Calvary, it was a small thing to strip and humble himself in the Upper Room.

A number of years ago there was a 'fad' among Christian young people to wear inexpensive wristbands (and perhaps some expensive ones too!) with the letters WWJD printed or etched on them. The letters stood for 'What Would Jesus Do?' Not all 'fads' are necessarily bad. There was certainly much that was good about this one, since Jesus is our example (John 13:13-15).

But perhaps a second wristband should have accompanied WWJD, this one with the letters WWJT: 'What Would Jesus *Think?*' Because doing what Jesus would do depends on having the mind of Christ, thinking the way Jesus thinks because we are united to him through his Spirit.

At the heart of our doing lies the style of our thinking. As we have already seen in these pages, 'the secret of holy living lies in the mind.'[1] That was true for Jesus himself. He expressed his cast of mind when he said, 'the Son of Man came not to be served but to serve, and to give his life as a ransom for many' (Matt. 20:28). In other words, Jesus' entire disposition was one of a willing servant of others.

What is so profoundly moving—and motivating—is that the Lord Jesus (yes, LORD!) was prepared to begin at the foot—at the feet of each of his disciples, including the betrayer.

If this is the way the Master went, should not the disciple follow him? Do you share the mind of Christ? Are you willing to begin at the foot? Remember it is the one who is faithful *in what is least* who is given the opportunity to be faithful in what is great (Luke 16:10).

Principles of service

The disciples must have watched transfixed as Jesus rose from his knees, replaced the basin of water and carefully folded the towel, replaced it, and then reached for his outer garment. Later perhaps it may have dawned on them that this was the last time any of them ever saw his back unscarred. Within hours his back would be bleed-

---

[1] John R. W. Stott, *Men Made New* (London: IVP, 1966) p. 50. Later, in his *Romans* (Downers Grove: IVP, 1994), p. 180, he repeats this conviction with a slight, but not unimportant, modification: 'The *major* secret of holy living is in the mind' (emphasis added).

ing, his hands and feet penetrated by nails, his side gashed open by a spear. But for this moment of time, through a drama that lasted only minutes, he was teaching them all what his crucifixion would mean.

Here was the dignity of Christ—the Lord of all—expressing the charity of Christ—his deep unselfish love; here was the humility of Christ—kneeling before those who were not worthy to sit at the same table with him—showing them the activity of Christ for their blessing—washing the dirt from their feet.

The Lord did not allow the moment to pass without comment. He still had so much to teach the disciples that they were not yet able to take in (John 16:12; does he feel the same about us?). But there was one thing they must learn immediately if they were going to be his disciples. If he washed their feet, they should wash one another's feet. As the Master lives, so must the servant live: 'I have given you an example, that you also should do just as I have done to you … If you know these things, blessed are you if you do them' (John 13:15, 17).

The New Testament uses different words that are translated 'example' in our English versions. John uses the Greek word *hupodeigma*. It means a sample, an illustration, a model which we should copy. The principle is simple: as Christians we belong to Jesus; he is our Elder Brother; we are called to follow his example.

But what does this mean when it comes to our service in and beyond the church family to which we belong? What are the principles?

We can put them both negatively and positively.

Negative 1: Service is not a matter of others recognizing our gifts.
Positive 1: Service is a matter of us recognizing others' needs.

Negative 2: Service is not a matter of doing things for others at our own convenience.
Positive 2: Service is a matter of us helping others when they are inconvenienced.

Negative 3: Service is not a matter of feeling we have special gifts.

Positive 3: Service is a matter of us seeing that others have very special needs.

Negative 4: Service is not an optional extra for a member of the church.

Positive 4: Service is written into the definition of being a member of the church.

If the Master washes the servants' feet, they must wash others' feet in turn. This is what it means to love. 'A new commandment I give to you,' said Jesus, 'that you love one another: *just as I have loved you*, you are also to love one another' (John 13:34). The kind of love he has in mind is not gauged by intensity of emotion but by the extent of our devotion, motivation, and action.

We sometimes say 'love is blind.' That may be true in some respects. But when the wisdom of Scripture seeps into our thinking, we develop something closer to 20/20 vision. Not only so, but in the fellowship of the love of the church family, as in our natural families, we learn by a kind of osmosis how to sense others' needs and to find ways of meeting them.

To be a Christian, then, to belong to the church, means to be willing and eager to serve, and then actually to serve. If you are not planning to serve in the life of a congregation, you should not be planning to join it!

When a person becomes part of any group there are principles of membership. Often these are spelled out in a membership handbook, or posted on a website. The more significant the association, the more detailed the membership book is likely to be. I still remember going to say good-night to one of our children at the end of the day he had become a new member of a golf club in our city (happy days in Scotland then, and still today, when the annual subscription for a youngster was less than a day's wages!). He was probably twelve or thirteen. I found him sitting up in bed with the Member's Handbook, reading every single clause with interest, care, and even enthusiasm. He was now a member. It all mattered to him. Wouldn't it be double-think on our part if we imagined that the church of Jesus Christ functioned without a handbook? It would be tragic if, having the best handbook in the world, the New Testament, we were to be indifferent to its most basic principles, such as:

> Love one another with brotherly affection. Outdo one another in showing honour. (Rom. 12:10)

In these pages we are trying to think through what some of these principles are. One of them is surely this: in committing yourself to the church you are committing yourself

(1) To the Lord of the church, Jesus Christ, and

(2) To the members of the church as fellow Christians.

To Christ we are called to give everything, without reservation. He has given his all for us; we are to give ourselves entirely to him, holding back nothing.

To our fellow members we are called to love. Here loving includes seeking to fulfil all the responsibilities of belonging together in fellowship. These include:

(1) Committing ourselves to never neglecting worship and fellowship on those occasions the church is called together as a whole, unless hindered by God's providence;

(2) Committing ourselves to prayer both individually and corporately for each other and for the extension of God's kingdom;

(3) Committing ourselves to serve our fellow believers, and to serve with them, employing the gifts God has given us for their blessing and for the sake of others.

Willingness to serve is not to be confused with high levels of 'activity' in the church. It has become a hallmark of church life today to flood the week with activities—sometimes to such a degree that it becomes impossible for the leaders of the fellowship to find space for the central activities. No, service is not the same as 'being active.' Much activity can give our churches a real sense of 'buzz.' That can be confused with, but it is not the same as, a real measure of spiritual growth. Service has much more to do with caring and loving than it has to do with merely being busy. So subtle are our sinful hearts that we can be constantly busy but in the process doing little more than serving our own interests. The test? The person who is genuinely busy in the Lord's work cares nothing about whether they are noticed or not, and whether they gain position in the church or not. For Christ-like servants are always taken up with the interests of others, not with their own.[1]

This is why elderly members can be just as much engaged in service as those who are more active and have more energy—a prayerful life, a listening ear, an open heart, shared wisdom, a short note of encouragement—these are often more fruitful forms of service than being the person who is always leading and being seen to be busy.

As John Milton's great sonnet 'On His Blindness' notes,

> They also serve who only stand and wait.

All this raises an important and frequently-asked question: How do I find my place to serve?

Finding your place

One of the potential blessings about being in a smaller congregation (unless, of course, there are unhealthy reasons why it is still small) is that there is room for all the gifts of all the members to be

---

[1] Paul urges this principle on the Philippian church, and in the process very beautifully gives examples of what it means—first of all in the Lord Jesus himself (Phil. 2:5-11) and then in Timothy and Epaphroditus (Phil. 2:19-29).

employed—from serving in the crèche to being part of the cleaning team, from teaching Sunday School to being part of the outreach. The problem is not finding a place to serve, but avoiding service-overload. The challenge of being over-small is that there may not be enough gifts and enough time for the church to function well.

In a larger church the challenge is very different. How in a membership of say 2,500 can everyone find a place to serve when the church seems already so well supplied with gifts?

Of course, part of the answer is: the larger the church the more need for you to serve.

But whether in small, medium, or large churches, each of us is still faced with the question, 'How do I find my place to serve here?'

Perhaps a caveat is in order at this point. It is not unusual in large churches to hear people say, 'This church is too large; I can't find a place to serve.'

In fact this is *never* true. And sadly, sometimes when such a statement is de-coded what it actually means is that the person feels they are not receiving the *recognition* they deserve. Complaining like this can become a very destructive heart murmur in the life of a fellowship. We are, after all, rarely under any compulsion to become members of large churches! And where they exist there are usually smaller churches around crying out for people to serve (since, sadly, some of their own complaining members have believed that the grass is greener in the larger church! But now, Exodus-Israelite like, they are complaining that when they were in Egypt they had cucumber to eat!). Do not complain about size when you should be opening your eyes to see the needs of others and how you could be meeting those needs.

How then can we go about finding a sphere of service? There are some simple principles that apply, whatever our gift may be, whatever our church family may be like. They are biblical principles; they always work; but they are also challenging.

Principle number one: *Be willing to do anything that needs to be done.* Just do it! 'If a thing is worth doing, it is worth doing well' goes the proverb. But it is also true that if it is worth doing, it is worth doing: 'Whatever your hand finds to do, do it with your might' (Eccles. 9:10). The person who is faithful in the small things will be entrusted with greater things. We need to learn to grow into the fellowship of the saints by serving them wherever we see a need—and in due course whatever particular gift or gifts the Lord has given to us will find their place and come to be increasingly appreciated and used.

This approach calls for humility, love for fellow believers, and a sense of yielding to the providence of God. He will give us plenty to do!

From time to time, however, Christians approach the leadership in a church in such terms as: 'If I were to become a member here would I be able to _____ [fill in the blank].' Often the blank is 'teach.'

Obviously those who ask this have no idea that it is usually a question calculated to make any wise leader nervous. There is something uncomfortably ego-centric rather than church-centred about it, isn't there? The idea that one would become a member of a fellowship on condition that there was a position of influence to occupy, or so that one could use one's 'gift'—rather than being willing simply to serve in whatever capacity would help—is often a warning sign that a person is more interested in themselves than they are in the fellowship. They are looking out more for their own gifts to be used than for Christ to be honoured and others helped.

John 13 encourages us to adopt 'the Jesus position' in the church family—to be on our knees washing the feet of our fellow believers, and others. The Christian who is willing to do whatever needs to be done is worth his or her weight in gold. That is why Paul said about Timothy, 'I have no one like him, who will be genuinely concerned for your welfare … But you know Timothy's proven worth … he has *served* with me in the gospel' (Phil. 2:20, 22).

Principle number two: *Seek to develop the graces that are essential to exercising your gifts for others.* If someone says, 'We really need to get A. B. to do X for us in the church' (where X might be anything from being the preacher, to ministering to the young people, or the women, or the children) there are two diagnostic questions wise leaders ask (sometimes employing them in disguised form!):

Question 1: Is this person really gifted for this ministry? We save ourselves both potential disaster and personal difficulties if we ask this right at the very beginning.

Think, for example, of the description Paul gives of the characteristic hallmarks of an elder. Is this person *able* to teach? There is only one proven way to answer that—when people are with him, or listen to him, they know they are learning from God's word. There may be various degrees of giftedness, of course. But the presence of the gift itself should not be in doubt.

Question 2: Is this person humble-minded towards us? Is he or she willing to serve? How sad it is sometimes in churches to hear a person with an argumentative rather than a servant spirit complain that his or her gifts are not being recognized!

These two qualities—giftedness and humility—are not the same. Giftedness without humility can be profoundly destructive. It tends to ego-centric activity rather than Christ-and-other-centred activity. It demeans others rather than builds them up. The use of a gift needs to be rooted in the graces necessary for the use of the gift simply because what happens when we use our gifts is that we are willing to become smaller so that others can grow taller and stronger! To state the biblical principle: *all the gifts of the Spirit require growth in all the fruit of the Spirit otherwise we grieve the Spirit.*

The Lord Jesus is our supreme model here. Paul sought to imitate him in his gift of preaching: 'For what we proclaim is not ourselves, but Jesus Christ as Lord, with ourselves as your servants for Jesus' sake' (2 Cor. 4:5). If only we took these words to heart, whatever our gift: Not ourselves … Jesus Christ as Lord … with ourselves your servants [the word is *doulos* which means a slave] for Jesus' sake.

Principle number three: *It is by serving, by doing whatever needs to be done, that space is created for the exercise of the gifts the Lord has given us for the church family.* If we serve the fellowship of Christ's people, they are blessed by them and instinctively want to see those gifts exercised to the full.

Christ does not give us gifts for ourselves, but for others. True, he does gift us so that we may not be blind, deaf, lame, paralyzed Christians who are incapable of serving. But the function of every spiritual gift we have is to enable us to say to our fellow Christians, 'The Lord Jesus has given me this FOR YOU.' We can never escape the call to 'the Jesus position': we kneel before him with empty hands and hearts and he fills them with graces and gifts; then we kneel before others and serve them.

So we will discover the gifts the Lord has given us—

- By sensing a concern to serve others and a desire to do it in particular ways. There is an inner compulsion.

- By serving.

- By experiencing the encouragement of others as they respond to our service, and by the way avenues seem to open up for us to continue to serve in these or other ways.

These are the three key elements Paul mentioned to Timothy in connection with his service:

I remind you to fan into flame the gift of God, which is in you through the laying on of my hands. (2 Tim. 1:6)

(1) God had given Timothy a gift.

(2) He was to show his own sense of that, and desire to use it by fanning it into flame in serving others.

(3) His giftedness had been recognized by the church fellowship through the laying on of hands by Paul (and others, 1 Tim. 4:14). In his case this was more formal; in ours it may well be quite informal—but either way the acceptance and encouragement we receive from the fellowship, the welcome of the church is one of the hallmarks of the presence of a gift.

Perhaps then we should be slightly more allergic than we often are to speaking about 'my gift' or its contemporary equivalent 'my gifting.' The New Testament nowhere joins the personal possessive pronoun 'my' to the word 'gift.' It does join it to the word 'ministry' or 'service.' The difference may seem slight, but it can be significant.

So, let us not be like Jesus' disciples in the Upper Room. They thought they were leaders (after all they argued about which of them was the greatest). They were above washing one another's feet. The paradox is that they were indeed to be leaders—but leaders formed in a different mould: *servant*-leaders. So first of all they needed to learn that the only leading position for Jesus' friends is the kneeling position.

We are no different, and so we learn to pray:

> May the mind of Christ, my Saviour,
>   Live in me from day to day,
> By His love and power controlling
>   All I do and say.
>
> May the word of God dwell richly
>   In my heart from hour to hour,
> So that all may see I triumph
>   Only through His power.

May the peace of God my Father
    Rule my life in everything,
That I may be calm to comfort
    Sick and sorrowing.

May the love of Jesus fill me
    As the waters fill the sea;
Him exalting, self abasing,
    This is victory.

May I run the race before me,
    Strong and brave to face the foe,
Looking only unto Jesus
    As I onward go

May His beauty rest upon me,
    As I seek the lost to win,
And may they forget the channel,
    Seeing only Him.

                    Katie Barclay Wilkinson (1859–1928)

10

Is There Anything Special for Supper?

or

Communion

Looking back I often feel amazed that my mother was so patient with me! I must have been an exasperation to her.

Regularly towards the end of the day I would ask her the same question: 'Is there anything *special* for supper?' (i.e. 'supper' in the Scots sense of something to eat shortly before going to bed).

My use of the word 'special' must have stretched the patience of my hard-working mother who was utterly devoted to her two boys. It implied 'something better than what we usually have' or 'something I particularly like.'

I learned, eventually, to stop asking the question! But the memory of asking it often comes back into my mind when I think of how we come to the service of the Lord's Supper. I find myself asking again, 'Is there anything *special* for supper?'

In this context it is a question worth asking.

Churches use a variety of terms to describe the service in which we re-enact part of the meal Jesus shared with his disciples just before his arrest: the 'Lord's Supper,' the 'Communion Service,' or the 'Eucharist.' They also celebrate it with different degrees of frequency—in some churches weekly, in others monthly, in yet others sometimes only twice a year. And there are different ways of conducting the service—in some the participants come to sit around a large single table, in others the whole church thinks of itself as seated together round the table at the front and are served from it, while in yet others people come forward in groups and receive the bread and the wine while standing.

Of course we can debate which of these ways of doing things is the most appropriate, or most faithful to Scripture—and Christians have done that now for centuries. But the single question we want to answer in this chapter is also the central one: 'Is there anything special for supper?' What are we doing when we receive the bread and the wine? What does it all mean? And what—if anything—is, or should be, in our minds when we eat the bread and drink the wine? We probably all experience what might be called 'the Peter Syndrome' in this context. Remember when Jesus was telling him that he, Simon Peter, would one day die for the sake of the gospel, he caught sight of the apostle John and said 'But what about ____?' In effect Jesus' response was, 'Peter, for the moment let's just concentrate on you, not on what anybody else does!'

Does anything 'happen'?

Imagine that, as you leave church one Sunday morning after the Lord's Supper, a television reporter puts his microphone in front of you, the camera behind him focuses on you, and he says, 'Can I ask you what you thought of the service? I believe you received the Lord's Supper. Can you tell us what happened? What did you think about during the service?'

What would you say? Would we all give the same answer—or at least approximately the same answer? Or is the Lord's Supper like so many other things in the church—we turn to the Bible to discover the message of salvation, or at least justification, but then tend to assume that for the rest we are essentially left to ourselves to sort out 'what works' in the church?

If we had been asked what happened when the Scriptures were being expounded in the service, most of us would be able to give a clear answer: the passage was read, its meaning was explained, its message was illustrated and applied to our lives, and as we listened we had a sense that God was speaking to us through his word.

But what about the Lord's Supper? What 'happens' then—if anything?

The Lord's Supper

The fullest explanation of the Lord's Supper is in Paul's first letter to the Corinthians.

The Corinthians, like most if not all of the earliest churches, met in private houses, perhaps several of them. They worshipped together on the first day of the week (1 Cor. 16:2); and when they gathered they shared meals together. Paul had heard that at these meals some of them were behaving in a disgraceful and unchristian way (1 Cor. 11:18-22). He comments vigorously on the way they were abusing their privileges and bringing shame on the gospel. But he is not only negative. He seizes the opportunity to teach them what the Lord's Supper really means—and therefore how different their attitude to it and to each other should be.

1 Corinthians 10:16-22

> The cup of blessing that we bless, is it not a participation in the blood of Christ? The bread that we break, is it not a participation in the body of Christ? Because there is one bread, we who are many are one body, for we all partake of the one bread. Consider the people of Israel: are not those who eat the sacrifices participants in the altar? What do I imply then? That food offered to idols is anything, or that an idol is anything? No, I imply that what pagans sacrifice they offer to demons and not to God. I do not want you to be participants with demons. You cannot drink the cup of the Lord and the cup of demons. You cannot partake of the table of the Lord and the table

of demons. Shall we provoke the Lord to jealousy? Are we stronger than he?

1 Corinthians 11:23-32

> For I received from the Lord what I also delivered to you, that the Lord Jesus on the night when he was betrayed took bread, and when he had given thanks, he broke it, and said, 'This is my body which is for you. Do this in remembrance of me.' In the same way also he took the cup, after supper, saying, 'This cup is the new covenant in my blood. Do this, as often as you drink it, in remembrance of me.' For as often as you eat this bread and drink the cup, you proclaim the Lord's death until he comes.
>
> Whoever, therefore, eats the bread or drinks the cup of the Lord in an unworthy manner will be guilty concerning the body and blood of the Lord. Let a person examine himself, then, and so eat of the bread and drink of the cup. For anyone who eats and drinks without discerning the body eats and drinks judgment on himself. That is why many of you are weak and ill, and some have died. But if we judged ourselves truly, we would not be judged. But when we are judged by the Lord, we are disciplined so that we may not be condemned along with the world.
>
> So then, my brothers, when you come together to eat, wait for one another—if anyone is hungry, let him eat at home—so that when you come together it will not be for judgment. About the other things I will give directions when I come.

What happens then when we come to the Lord's Table? We can summarize Paul's teaching in a few words:

1. *Communion*

The most important fact to know about the Lord's Supper is that Jesus Christ himself is present with us when we receive the bread and wine from the table.

Paul says that as we eat and drink we have 'participation' in the body and blood of Christ (1 Cor. 10:16, 17). The word he uses is one of those Greek words that most Christians have heard sometime or another—*koinōnia*, 'fellowship.'

But what does it mean to have fellowship in Christ's body and blood? Isn't this one of the major problem areas and a point of disagreement among Christians? How can we be expected to provide a solution?

But perhaps it is not so complicated after all. Think of the famous words of Jesus which John took down by dictation and then wrote to the church in Laodicaea:

> Behold, I stand at the door and knock. If anyone hears my voice and opens the door, I will come in to him and eat with him, and he with me. (Rev. 3:20)

When did Jesus ever sup with the Christians in Laodicaea? Don't you think this is a perfect description of the Lord's Supper? Yes, these words have often been used as an evangelistic text, as an appeal to people who are not yet Christians. But they were first spoken to a church of professing Christians. They needed to sense their sinfulness and failure, the lukewarmness of their hearts, and repent. They needed to come near to Christ all over again. But that is exactly what we are invited to do at the Lord's Supper! Jesus is describing what we will experience as we come to him in faith while we are receiving the bread and the wine. We will 'sup' with him, and he will 'sup' with us.

These words then are a beautiful description of what happens at the Lord's Supper. We receive into our hands physical emblems of 'Jesus Christ and him crucified'; we take them, indeed we take them into ourselves, and by faith we receive the love the Lord Jesus expresses. Although he is invisible to us he expresses his love for us by giving these tangible gifts to us to remind us of who he is and what he has done; they carry the message 'I have loved you so much that I was willing to die for you. I am present with you now as your risen Saviour and Friend. Take these love-gifts from me.'

We not only symbolize but actually express our commitment, our love, by a handshake or a kiss—a physical expression of a spiritual reality which is able to communicate the reality. The same is true of the Supper. There, by his Spirit, the Lord Jesus comes to us. He gives us these visible and tangible signs of his love and his presence, just as in the preaching he does this by verbal and audible signs. We in turn come to him, through the same Spirit, and have supper with him.

The invitation to the Lord's Supper then, is an invitation to be with Jesus, and to have communion with him.

2. *Reconciliation*

There is a special focus at the Lord's Supper. Christ makes himself known to us in a particular way at the Table in the breaking and eating of the bread, and in the drinking of the outpoured wine. Here at the Table our focus is not on his birth, or on his wonderful miracles, or even on his teaching, although all of that is implied. It is on Jesus himself as the one who was crucified for us, who died for our sins under God's judgment, and who is now risen and glorified—but who brings us into his presence, near to him, to have fellowship with him through the Spirit.

Here then our focus is on the great exchange which lies at the heart of the gospel—Christ took what was ours (sin, guilt, shame, and death) in order that by faith we might receive what was his (fellowship with his heavenly Father). He has 'raised us up with him and seated us with him in the heavenly places in Christ Jesus' (Eph. 2:6). That is exactly what happens at the Lord's Supper. He took our sin and judgment so really and fully that he cried out on the cross 'I thirst!' We are invited to sit with him and hear him say, 'No longer be hungry, or thirsty. Here—eat this bread; drink this cup.'

This full reconciliation we receive in Christ has a profound impact on our relationships with each other. As the early Christians gathered in relatively small meetings they almost certainly used a single loaf and a single common cup as they shared in the Supper. Paul commented on the symbolism of this—we eat from one loaf and drink from one cup because we are one body in Christ, members of one family. We are united together both in Christ and because of Christ.

So just as the Lord's Supper expresses our reconciliation to God through Jesus Christ, it also expresses our reconciliation to one another as one body in Christ. That is one reason Christians in antiquity greeted each other with 'the peace' ('The peace of the Lord Jesus Christ be with you'). One of the real signs that we have experienced everything Christ offers us at the Table is that when we rise from it we want to love the fellow Christians who surround us, and be reconciled to any of them from whom we may have become estranged. In this way the Lord's Supper melts hard hearts, encourages us to forgive others, and creates a wonderful fresh spirit of fellowship.

3. *Proclamation*

Jesus taught the apostles (who in turn taught the whole church) to 'do this' (i.e. 'keep on doing this') in memory of him. What is it that we 'do in memory' of Christ? Paul explains when he says: 'as often as you eat this bread and drink the cup, you proclaim the Lord's death until he comes' (1 Cor. 11:26).

Sometimes this has been read as if Paul were saying: 'Don't ever have the Lord's Supper without having a sermon.' Of course, it is always helpful for us to come to the Lord's Table with minds informed and hearts warmed by the preaching of God's word, especially when it has been centred on Christ himself.

But Paul is not speaking about the necessity of a sermon being preached *before* we come to the Table. Rather he is saying that what happens *at the Table* is a sermon. It is a proclamation of Jesus Christ crucified for our sins, raised again to be with us as our Lord, Saviour, Host and Friend. This is why some Christians have spoken of the Supper as a 'visible word.' Just as in the sermon Christ is proclaimed by audible words, in the Supper, what he has done for us is proclaimed in symbols—bread broken, wine outpoured. Here the gospel is being proclaimed in dramatic form—as our forefathers used to say, not only to ear-gate, but to eye-gate.

In fact not only the gospel message but the nature of a true response to the gospel is enacted when we celebrate the Supper.

For one thing—at least in my own church tradition, which in this instance I believe best mirrors the Scriptures—it is not necessarily a minister or an elder (or leader) who serves us. Even if the elders or leaders bring the bread and wine from the table to us, *we all serve each other*. We are proclaiming the gospel to one another! Our hands are saying, even if our lips do not form the words: 'Take, eat. Take, drink! Christ has died for us and risen again. Enjoy communion with him as through my hands he gives you these gifts; and then proclaim him to your neighbour.' At the Table we all preach the gospel!

4. Benediction

Doesn't the 'benediction' come at the end of the service? Well, we trust that there will be benediction, or blessing, all the way through the service! But have you noticed how it is especially part of the Lord's Supper?

Paul calls the cup, 'the cup of blessing that we bless' (1 Cor. 10:16). What does he mean? Why is the cup which is a symbol and expression of blessing, also itself a benediction?

'Bless' is a word that has, over time, lost much of its meaning. Nowadays almost the only context in which we hear it is when someone sneezes and people say in response, 'Bless you!' And then there are some areas in the English-speaking world where the expression 'bless him' is used at the end of the description of someone usually with the implication, 'Poor fellow; he tries his best, but he's not up to much and he doesn't really know how to do any better.'

That use is almost a diameter removed from what 'bless' means in the Bible. But, perhaps surprisingly the fact that we say 'Bless you!' when someone sneezes actually points us back to its original meaning.

Do you know why we say 'Bless you!' when someone sneezes?

It is a tradition that may reach back to the Middle Ages and the days when the Bubonic Plague devastated Europe. One of the symptoms of contracting the plague was sneezing. It is possible that the nursery game and rhyme 'A ring, a ring of roses, a pocket full of posies, "atishoo!" "atishoo!" we all fall down' reflects this background. When teachers or parents play this game with children they are usually quite oblivious to the fact that it is a 'death game'! 'Atishoo'—first sneezing (the symptom of the plague); then 'we all fall down' (that is, fall down dead). A rather macabre game for children!

But why say 'Bless you!'? Because the plague was viewed in the Middle Ages as a mark of God's curse. In Scripture the word 'bless' is the opposite of the word 'curse.' The former describes a situation in which God's grace and covenant salvation have come into play, the latter describes a situation where his judgment has come. The words 'Bless you' were the short form of the prayer 'May the Lord bless you …' In other words, 'May God's curse be turned away from you and may you instead experience his blessing and salvation.'

It is in this sense that the cup at Communion is 'the cup of blessing.' Jesus gave it to his disciples in the Upper Room. But then he went out to the Garden of Gethsemane and took the cup of divine curse from his Father's hand. 'Shall I not drink the cup that the Father has given me?' he said to Simon Peter (John 18:11).

What did this cup contain? Jesus knew the Scriptures that described its contents and the effect of drinking it:

Psa. 75:8: For in the hand of the LORD there is a cup with foaming wine, well mixed, and he pours out from it, and all the wicked of the earth shall drain it down to the dregs.

Isa. 51:17: Wake yourself, wake yourself, stand up, O Jerusalem, you who have drunk from the hand of the LORD the cup of his wrath, who have drunk to the dregs the bowl, the cup of staggering.

Jer. 25:15-18: Thus the LORD, the God of Israel, said to me: 'Take from my hand this cup of the wine of wrath, and make all the nations to whom I send you drink it. They shall drink and stagger and be crazed because of the sword that I am sending among them.' So I took the cup from the LORD's hand, and made all the nations to whom the LORD sent me drink it: Jerusalem and the cities of Judah, its kings and officials, to make them a desolation and a waste, a hissing and a curse, as at this day.

Christ drank the contents of this cup—the wrath of God against the world's sin. He did so—for us. Because of this he was able to offer the cup of blessing to his disciples—and now also to us.

As we come to the Table, then, we know that the cup of God's curse upon our sin has been drained to its last bitter dregs. It is empty. Now we are being graciously offered the cup of blessing in its place.

No wonder the words of the psalmist have often been used at the Lord's Supper:

What shall I render to the LORD for all his benefits towards me? I will take the cup of salvation, and call upon the name of the LORD.

(Psa. 116:12)

5. Consecration

Paul has this in view in his comments in 1 Corinthians 10:16-22.

Corinth was an idol-saturated city. Just as today people might 'drink a toast' to a bride and bridegroom expressing a desire for their happiness, so drink offerings—toasts we might call them—were made to the 'gods' represented by these idols. This was simply part and parcel of civic life in Corinth. You were expected to participate, certainly if you wanted to get ahead in life. So, *not to participate* in these feasts was not something that happened by accident. It was regarded as tantamount to condemning them. There was intense pressure on Christians to compromise—just to go along, to share in the toasts.

But Paul says to the Corinthians: You cannot live with one foot in each camp. You cannot drink the cup of the blessing of Christ and then go and drink the cup consecrated to idols. If you belong to that world you cannot belong to Christ—and vice versa.

It was a simple choice.

It was also a costly choice.

It is also the choice we are called to make every time we sit at the Lord's Supper and receive the bread and the wine. Will you live entirely and exclusively for the One who died for you—or under the influence of the world that has rejected him?

If we eat and drink in the presence of Christ we are telling him (and each other) that we have made the decision—all that remains is that we keep it when we leave the Table. What we see on the Table encourages us: bread to be broken, wine to be poured out. He died for me—I will give my life to him!

And we make that choice knowing the blessing of the presence of Christ with us at the Table.

Psalm 23 is therefore wonderfully appropriate for us to meditate on when we sit together to take the Lord's Supper:

> You prepare a table before me
>   in the presence of my enemies;
> You anoint my head with oil;
>   my cup overflows.
> Surely goodness and mercy shall follow me
>   all the days of my life,
> And I shall dwell in the house of the LORD
>   forever. (Psa. 23:5, 6)

6. Anticipation

At the Lord's Supper we 'proclaim the Lord's death *until he comes*' (1 Cor. 11:26). Yes, as we come to the Table we seek the presence of Christ with us now; we look back to his death for us; and we also look up to heaven where he has ascended. But in addition we look forward to his return.

We will not celebrate the Lord's Supper forever. It will give way, one day, to the marriage supper of the Lamb described so vividly in Revelation 21–22. The Supper reminds us that we are called now to live looking forward to that day.

In this sense too, the Lord's Supper is a miniature drama of the whole Christian life.

The New Testament tells us that we live between two great events, Christ's first coming in humility to deal with sin, and his second coming in majesty to reign in eternal glory (Heb. 9:28). We have *already* been set free from the guilt and reign of sin and Satan by Christ's death and resurrection. But we have *not yet* been set free from the presence and influence of sin. And so we are called to persevere in our pilgrimage, to keep fighting the Christian warfare, and to do so wearing spiritual armour (Eph. 6:10-20).

How does the Lord's Supper help us? It is a foretaste of what is yet to come. The invisible presence of Christ with us assures us of the glory that his visible presence will bring. Although we do not see him, says Peter, we love him (1 Pet. 1:8). But one day we will see him face to face, and then there will be no bounds to our love and joy.

In the United Kingdom the night before a wedding is often a time for the bride and groom to be apart and with their own nuclear family for one last occasion. The reception following the wedding has traditionally been the financial responsibility of the bride's father. In the United States a different tradition has developed—the wedding rehearsal dinner. After the final rehearsal, both families and their friends will dine together—traditionally at the expense of the groom's father!

Think of the Lord's Supper as a wedding rehearsal dinner—at the expense of the Groom's Father. The next thing on the calendar is the return of the Saviour and the marriage supper of the Lamb. But for the moment we are guests at the rehearsal dinner. The Groom is present, the church is his bride. The Father of the Groom undertakes to provide everything that will give us joy as we look forward to the wedding day that is coming.

Here at the Table everything is in miniature. But one day all will be revealed. That is why we rise from the Lord's Table with a renewed longing to be faithful until the day of Christ dawns and all the shadows flee away and we see him face to face. Then his prayer for us will be answered: 'Father, I desire that they also, whom you have given me, may be with me where I am, to see my glory that you have given me because you loved me before the foundation of the world' (John 17:24).

What a day that will be! But in the meantime, Peter tells us—

> Though you have not seen him,
> you love him.
> Though you do not now see him,
> you believe in him and
> rejoice with joy that is inexpressible
> and filled with glory. (1 Pet. 1:8)

No better description of the joy of communion with Christ could be penned.

Communion, Reconciliation, Benediction, Proclamation, Consecration, Anticipation—these words sum up the meaning of the Supper for us. Think of it in terms of any single one of them, or any combination of them, and its meaning will become clearer to you. And as you focus on how Christ makes himself known to you in these ways, coming to the Lord's Table will mean more and more to you.

But there is one further word we need to notice.

7. Self-Examination

Because there was disorder in the lives of some of the Corinthians, Paul told them to examine themselves before they came to the Table.

No one should come to the Lord's Table 'unworthily.' Paul does not imply that anyone is morally 'worthy' to come to Christ. He means that the way we come to the Supper needs to be consistent with its significance. If we come while behaving in a manner that contradicts the gospel, then we are 'guilty of profaning the body and blood of the Lord' (1 Cor. 11:27). For by our actions at the Table we are saying that Christ means everything to us, but by the way we live our lives we are saying that Christ means nothing to us.

So each person who comes must 'examine himself' and come 'discerning the body' (1 Cor. 11:29). Paul may be speaking here about understanding the meaning of the bread and the wine, and recognizing that they come to us as an expression of the presence and love of the Saviour who died for us. Or he may mean that we need to realize that at the Supper we are gathered as the one body of Jesus Christ and therefore to be alienated from each other is to be alienated from Christ.

In one sense each implies the other. In either case the danger is that our lives contradict what is being proclaimed at the Table.

But then Paul adds some sobering words. If we do not come in faith to Christ at the Table, we nevertheless do not thereby leave unaffected. Far from it. We drink judgment on ourselves (1 Cor. 11:29). For we have ignored or spurned the One who is represented by, and offered to us in, the bread and the wine. We have thus despised the blessing of the One who bore God's curse for us. We therefore have no one else but ourselves to bear the curse for us. We must bear it ourselves.

Perhaps it was this kind of response to the Supper that the author of Hebrews also had in mind when he wrote:

If we deliberately keep on sinning after we have received the knowledge of the truth, no sacrifice for sins is left, but only a fearful expectation of judgment and of raging fire that will consume the enemies of God. Anyone who rejected the law of Moses died without mercy on the testimony of two or three witnesses. How much more severely do you think a man deserves to be punished who has trampled the Son of God under foot, who has treated as an unholy thing the blood of the covenant that sanctified him, and who has insulted the Spirit of grace? (Heb. 10:26-29)

But when we come in faith we experience the joy of the same author's earlier words:

Therefore, brothers, since we have confidence to enter the holy places by the blood of Jesus, by the new and living way that he opened for us through the curtain, that is, through his flesh, and since we have a great priest over the house of God, let us draw near with a true heart in full assurance of faith, with our hearts sprinkled clean from an evil conscience and our bodies washed with pure water. Let us hold fast the confession of our hope without wavering, for he who promised is faithful. And let us consider how to stir up one another to love and good works, not neglecting to meet together, as is the habit of some, but encouraging one another, and all the more as you see the Day drawing near. (Heb. 10:19-25)

11

Home and Away

or

Christian Witness and World Mission

New life in Christ seems to change everything, not least because it gives us a new purpose for living—'to glorify God and to enjoy him for ever' as the Westminster Shorter Catechism expresses it so well. Everything in life is now redirected. Christ transforms even the details. And Christ calls us to be a 'witness' to him.

When Jesus promised that the Holy Spirit would come to serve as a witness to him (John 15:26) he told the disciples that this would be their task too: 'You also will bear witness, because you have been with me from the beginning' (John 15:27). Later, in his parting words in the Great Commission (Matt. 28:18-20) he told them that they were to be witnesses throughout the world, and promised that as they did so he would be with them. They in turn were to teach the church to do everything he had commanded them. That included being witnesses to him. Obedient Christians, faithful church members are therefore, by definition, witnesses.

We are so familiar with Christians using this term that we can forget that it is not a distinctively *Christian* word. It had a legal background. It belonged—as it still does—to the world of the law court. This is highlighted especially in John's Gospel, where Jesus is portrayed as being on trial before the world, while John, as it were, calls a series of witnesses to testify to Jesus' identity. Jesus is still on trial before a watching world. And just as juries decide verdicts on the basis of the evidence of witnesses, so we provide evidence for Jesus as Son of God, Saviour, and Lord.

Simon Peter's first letter, originally written to Christians in modern day Turkey is, in some ways, a basic manual for Christian discipleship and witnessing in difficult days. He describes some of the contexts in which we are to be witnesses: personal life, civic life, married life, working life, even (indeed especially) persecuted life. In all of them, he says, always

> be ready to give a defence [a reason, an answer or explanation] for the hope that is in you. (1 Pet. 3:15)

However, there is an interesting difference between Peter's *Manual for Witnessing to Christ* and its modern counterparts. Modern manuals generally assume that we need to learn how to open up 'gospel conversations' with non-Christians. Sometimes groups of Christians have resorted to asking people to respond to a questionnaire in the hope of prompting questions and conversations about Christ.

Peter does not take that approach. Indeed he does not really share the same assumptions. He assumes that non-Christians will be the ones who ask questions of Christians. Indeed he seems to assume this is inevitable. Therein lies the difference. How so? Is this significant? Almost certainly.

I owned my first evangelism manual when I was sixteen. I think I can still remember how it began—by reassuring me I could witness to anybody. Thus the first page told me I could even open up a conversation with a man who was casually walking his dog. Do you know how to do that? You go up to him and say, 'Excuse me, sir, but that is a fine dog you have. Did you know that "dog" is "God" spelled backwards?' Of course there are some people who can, as we say, 'get away with murder'—but that does not make their practices universal principles! In the parts of the city where I was trying to be a witness for Christ, telling a man that 'dog' was 'God' spelled backwards would probably not have elicited an encouraging response! But apart from other considerations, techniques like this are contrived and unnatural.

In the early church it was Christians who were being asked questions.[1] Their lives demanded explanation! Why were they so different? What did it mean to become a follower of Jesus?

Why this difference between the first century and the twenty-first century?

What makes non-Christians ask questions?

Peter implies that non-Christians would ask about 'the hope that is in you.' It was a visible reality in the lives of these early Christians:

> Blessed be the God and Father of our Lord Jesus Christ! According to his great mercy, he has caused us to be born again to a living hope through the resurrection of Jesus Christ from the dead, to an inheritance that is imperishable, undefiled, and unfading, kept in heaven for you, who by God's power are being guarded through faith for a salvation ready to be revealed in the last time. In this you rejoice, though now for a little while, if necessary, you have been grieved by various trials, so that the tested genuineness of your faith—more precious than gold that perishes though it is tested by fire—may be found to result in praise and glory and honour at the revelation of Jesus Christ. Though you have not seen him, you love him. Though you do not now see him, you believe in him and rejoice with joy that is inexpressible and filled with glory, obtaining the outcome of your faith, the salvation of your souls. (1 Pet. 1:3-9)

What, then, had non-Christians noticed? It was their *hope*, that is their assurance of their salvation in Christ and the joy it created.

---

[1] We see that in such passages as Acts 2:37; 8:30-31; 16:30.

They seemed like people who had been born all over again into a life of confidence in their relationship to God, and a certainty that their sins had been forgiven. They knew God. Doubtless this was expressed quietly in some of them and more exuberantly in others. But their new sense of purpose, their remarkable peace could not be hidden. The 'hope' of which Peter writes was not mere 'wishful thinking,' but a strong assurance of God's grace. This can never be hidden, even when Christians are not conscious that they are expressing it. Non-Christians have no explanation for what they are seeing.

There was also a new *power* in their lives—they were 'kept by the power of God.' This was the explanation of their peace and poise in times of stress and trial, and their godly character in an ungodly world. They resisted temptation simply because they wanted to serve the Lord Jesus and become like him. Their friends could not understand why their pattern of life had changed: they were 'surprised' by it (1 Pet. 4:4).

In addition, people who are not Christians are often puzzled by the *love for Jesus* that is such a hallmark of Christian faith—even although we have never seen him (1 Pet. 1:8). To them 'Christ' is a word heard only as an exclamation not as adoration. Since they do not know him they cannot love him. But they see that we know him and love him. It surprises them that he is the Someone we love best of all. Our friendships and marriages, our homes and families are something of a puzzle to them. There is something there they simply cannot work out!

The hidden agenda that shapes our lives as Christians is loving, honouring, enjoying, and serving Jesus Christ. But the non-Christian knows nothing about that. Yet the difference is bound to show since what Peter calls 'joy that is inexpressible and filled with glory' cannot be hidden (1 Pet. 1:8). It takes different shapes and forms as it weaves its way into our individual personalities and lives, but it is present in every believer. There is a peace that passes all understanding that guards our hearts and minds (Phil. 4:7). We know that the Lord Jesus reigns over us and all of our circumstances—even in times of trial (1 Pet. 1:6, 7; James 1:2). That inevitably contrasts with what non-Christians mean when they talk about 'having a good time'! It is completely beyond the experience of non-Christians—that is why it is strange, even puzzling to them—as John Newton taught the church to sing, 'Solid joys and lasting treasure none but Zion's children know'![1]

Such lives inevitably provoke questions, spoken or unspoken. It seems strange to non-Christians; they have never seen anything quite like it (1 Pet. 2:11); they cannot understand it; it perplexes them.

This reality is well expressed in the interesting metaphor Peter uses to describe Christians. We are 'exiles' (1 Pet. 2:11). This world is not our homeland. Paul develops this further when he tells the Christians in Philippi (a Roman colony, whose citizens therefore had Roman citizenship) that their permanent citizenship is in heaven (Phil. 3:20).

My native country is Scotland. For many years I lived and worked in the United States. Strangers have often said to me, 'You have an accent.' (Sometimes I have replied, 'No, you are the one who has the accent!' only to receive the reply, 'No, *I* don't have an accent—but *you* do!')

Sometimes people fail to recognize my country of origin ('Are you German?' 'Irish?' 'English?'). But even if they cannot place the accent they know I am 'not from around here.' There is something about an accent that puzzles or intrigues people enough for them to try to identify it—where does this person come from?

Christians have an accent too.

---

[1] From the hymn by John Newton (1725–1807), 'Glorious things of thee are spoken.'

One well-known difference between the way Scots and Americans speak—even although the same language is being used—is that the accent is sometimes placed on a different syllable. Sometimes the spelling may be slightly different—just enough for haughty people from the United Kingdom to complain that Americans don't spell some English words properly. Same word, different accent, or different spelling. But the difference tends to stick out. You cannot but notice it. This is what the New Testament is telling us about Christians and their witness—our accent is different, we spell out the story of our lives differently, even though we live in the same world. And it prompts non-Christians to wonder, 'Where is he from?' 'What makes her tick?'

Wherever this is so, non-Christians are prompted to ask questions.

Yes, of course it is still true that we need to find ways of expressing and communicating our faith. But the best way is when a changed life, devotion to Jesus Christ, deep assurance and real joy so mark our lives that others ask us questions first.

But it is one thing for our lives to provoke questions. How are we to answer them when they arise?

Answers

Our witness to the world is seen in both word and action.

In our words

Peter urged his Christian brothers and sisters always to be 'prepared to make a defence to any who asks for a reason for the hope that is in you' (1 Pet. 3:15). The word translated 'defence' here is *apologia*. We derive the English word 'apology' from it, by which we usually mean 'to say sorry' for some misdeed. But its more basic meaning is to give a reasoned explanation for something. Thus, for example, when John Henry Newman, the nineteenth-century Anglican minister who became a Roman Catholic and eventually a cardinal, entitled his autobiography *Apologia Pro Sua Vita*, he was not apologizing for his life but explaining it. This is what we mean when, on the basis of 1 Peter 3:15 we engage in what we call Christian Apologetics. This goes back to the classical use of *apologia* in a court context—a speech made for the defence. Paul uses it in this sense when he speaks about the 'defence and confirmation of the gospel' (Phil. 1:7 and again in 1:16).[1] So we engage in apologetics whenever we give a reasoned explanation of our faith. We are to 'tell the truth, the whole truth, and nothing but the truth' about Christ and the Christian faith. Peter tells us that we must always be ready to do this.

This does not mean we should try to memorize a set of formulas. It is not because we have learned the script that we will succeed as witnesses. But we do need to study and think through the biblical teaching about the gospel, and to develop an ability to answer basic questions about it. As we do we will be equipped to listen to what others say to us, and respond to them by articulating the main points of the gospel, explaining what Scripture has to say about the human condition, about who Christ is, what he has done, why we need him, how to trust in him and what is involved in following him. We should also seek to grow in our ability to *defend* the faith, confident that while it describes supernatural events it is not irrational.

But there is a second element:

In our actions

Christian witness also needs to be expressed in our lifestyle. Peter calls us to explain and defend the gospel with 'gentleness [or meekness] and respect [*phobos*].' Is this respect God-directed or other-directed? Perhaps it is both. Those who bow before God's word and ways

---

[1] In the Acts of the Apostles the verb is used in Acts 19:33; 24:10; 26:24 while the noun occurs in Acts 22:1; 25:16. Paul himself uses it in 2 Tim. 4:16 of his 'first defence' during his court appearances in Rome.

in meekness will be sensitive to anything that would cause him to frown. Their meekness (not weakness) will also make an impression on others. It leads them to show respect for others, even although they are not Christians, because they have been created in the image of God (Gen. 1:26-28).

Such meekness and sensitivity were not prized virtues in antiquity any more than they are today. But for that very reason they stand out as counter-cultural. But more than that, these characteristics are the direct fruit of the gospel's transforming power, since they are reflections of the character of the Lord Jesus. They serve as pointers to him. Thus our words about Christ along with our Christ-reflecting actions and dispositions are used by the Spirit to point others to Christ. The truth of the gospel is explained in our words and illustrated in our actions. We thus 'adorn the doctrine of God our Saviour' (Titus 2:10).

This cannot be emphasized too strongly. How much damage has been done by people whose lives contradicted their Christian profession; how much blessing has been brought by Christians whose lives have shone with gospel beauty! In this connection I often remember the dated, but moving language of a letter written in 1843 to a twenty-nine year old Scottish minister, thanking him for his preaching:

> I heard you preach last Sabbath evening, and it pleased God to bless that sermon to my soul. It was not so much what you said, as your manner of speaking that struck me. I saw in you a beauty in holiness that I never saw before.[1]

The young Scottish minister was Robert Murray M'Cheyne; the letter addressed lay still unopened on his desk on the day of his death. Time and time again we learn that this is how the Spirit 'speaks' through our lives.

---

[1] Alexander Smellie, *Robert Murray M'Cheyne* (London: National Council of Evangelical Free Churches, 1913), p. 204.

Sometimes people say to me, 'I have read some of your books. But this is the first time I have heard you preach. Now I will be able to hear your accent when I read them!' In a sense that is what happens when our words and our lives unite to bear witness to Christ. Having seen what Christ has done in our lives they begin to understand that he is the same person who is described in, and speaks through, the Scriptures. Once they make the connection, they may begin to seek Christ for themselves.

There are many reasons why this is important. But one of the most neglected is this: when a church has not seen anyone converted for a prolonged period of time its conviction that God calls people into his kingdom tends to become more of an intellectual assent than an experienced reality. Both expectation and prayer that people will be brought to faith as they come in contact with our church family are weakened, But when someone is converted, then both prayer and expectation leap into life. We begin to feel ourselves caught up in the ongoing work of the Spirit. The whole church begins to feel that springtime has come and new life is emerging—since new babies are being born into the kingdom of God. The fellowship of the church family becomes the thrilling reality it was meant to be.

That is surely what we want to see in the churches to which we belong!

This point underlines a feature of the New Testament church we have already considered—the tendency to individualize and privatize our evangelism—so much so that it is often referred to as 'personal evangelism.' It is a frequently overstated fact that in the New Testament the second person pronoun ('you') is characteristically plural and not singular; but while *what is written* is 'you' plural *what is heard* is usually 'you' singular. Thus exhortations to the community are truncated as though they were addressed only to individuals. The church needs to hear these exhortations as addressed to each and all of us as a fellowship. It is as the church family that we are called to be a witness to Christ. We are a city set on a hill; we are to be salt together, not single grains. Evangelism therefore needs to be seen as a corporate activity in which each member of the entire church family has a role to play.

Some 'evangelistic programmes' take no account of this. Others do, sometimes even although the 'programme' was not first conceived with this specifically in view. In a well-structured church family these corporate activities will always be given an important place.

To use one example, a multi-week 'course' or 'programme' like *Christianity Explored*© can be used in the context of a preliminary meal or food and refreshments served by members of the church. This provides an opportunity for natural, genuine informal conversation about the gospel, but also to meet with Christians as a fellowship and family. In this way non-Christians can see for themselves the new life produced by the gospel and the new community that has been shaped by the gospel. This is a powerful witnessing combination. An added benefit is that Christians who feel they are not well-equipped to speak for Christ find other ways of serving. As they do so, and listen to and watch more mature Christians explain and defend the gospel, often they themselves are drawn in to witness to Christ in word as well as in deed.

In the first century A.D., the whole church was an evangelistic instrument. The kind of fellowship experienced in it, the mutual love and care, were unique in the pre-Christian era. It remains so in the post-Christian era. Today individual spiritual experience may not make the same impact as it did when people in general had a better grasp of the Bible's message. That can no longer be anticipated in a world where writing that someone has been 'born again' is as likely to appear on the sports pages as in the religious columns of our newspapers. Today people are 'converted' from all manner of backgrounds in which religion tends to be profoundly self-centred and subjective, but the world can remain relatively unimpressed by individual conversion. 'If that works for others, so be it,' it says, 'but it is not for me.'

However, the new community of grace, the counter-cultural fellowship, the church family that Christ has created—this cannot be paralleled or imitated. Here people can see how life together should be lived, and what real family life is—and be prompted to seek an explanation for what they both see and feel. Not only so, but when our church family is working together even the timid can find a role (we can all say, 'Would you like some more coffee?'). Over time we will find ourselves progressing from our faltering first steps in speaking to strangers about food and drink to speaking to them about our Saviour. After all, one of Jesus' most remarkable evangelistic conversations began with him asking for a drink of water.[1]

So what should we learn from this? Simply that if there is an opportunity to share in a fellowship outreach like this, even if we feel nervous, we should step out in faith with our arms linked to our fellow believers. We will then discover the joy of serving and we will grow in our ability to be a witness by our words as well as by our actions. As we reflect on Peter's teaching we should notice two details of what he says. The first is that Christian witness comes from hearts that 'regard Christ the Lord as holy' and it is marked by 'gentleness and respect' (1 Pet. 3:15).

But our calling is bigger than even this. We are called not only to be a witness where we live, work, and play. We are summoned to be world Christians.

Missions

The Edinburgh World Missions Conference held in 1910 was one of the most famous missionary conferences in history—so famous that its hundredth anniversary in 2010 was marked by another conference. The slogan of the original conference was 'The evangelism of

---

[1] John 4:7.

the world in our time.' But about it one of the leading historians of world missions in our times, Professor Andrew Walls, could later write:

> It has passed into Christian legend. It was a landmark in history of mission; starting point of the modern theology of mission; the high point of the Western missionary movement and the point from which it declined.[1]

What has happened? Has the earth become such a global village that missions beyond our own lands have become redundant? Are we more enlightened about the status of those who have never heard the gospel, or who have not responded to it in faith? Have we lost zeal? Or is a rose still a rose by any other name? Do 'world missions' continue to be an important aspect of the church's *raison d'être*, but now appearing in a different guise, not in church missions boards and committees, or in missionary societies and organizations, but simply in the way Christians sense a call to work overseas in their different vocations as craftsmen, teachers, physicians, lawyers, financial experts—and a hundred other professions?

It is always a good idea to begin at the beginning. But where is the beginning of world missions? From one point of view the answer is actually 'at creation!' For it was then that God's people were given a worldwide mission. In a sense God had first given Adam a local mission—to tend the garden in which he had set him (Gen. 2:8, 15). But he had also given him a wider task. Since there was much that was 'not yet garden,' Adam and Eve were called to reflect the God who had created and cared for all things and so they were told, 'Be fruitful and multiply and fill the earth and subdue it …' (Gen. 1:28). The reign of God in and through their lives locally was to be extended until the earth would be 'filled with the knowledge of the glory of the Lord as the waters cover the sea' (Hab. 2:14). Their mission

---

[1] Andrew F. Walls, *The Cross-Cultural Process in Christian History* (Maryknoll, NY: Orbis Books), p. 53.

was to turn the whole earth into a garden, the little temple in which they met with God was to be enlarged to take in everything.

That was a real mission; it was a transforming mission; but it was not a redemptive mission. That second mission would come after their disobedience and fall—in the life and death of the second man and last Adam, God's Son Jesus Christ.

This new mission was gradually revealed also to be worldwide in scope. Redemption would come through the offspring of Adam and Eve (Gen. 3:15). But then it became clearer: in Abraham's seed all the nations of the earth would be blessed:

> I will make you a great nation, and I will bless you and make your name great, so that you will be a blessing. I will bless those who bless you … and in you all the families of the earth shall be blessed.
>
> (Gen. 12:1-3)

'Family' in this context does not mean 'nuclear family,' although it no doubt includes that. It extends to the idea of a tribe, a clan, even an entire people-group. That promised 'blessing'—the removal of the divine judgment curse, and the gift of new life—would eventually be fulfilled in the coming of Christ as God's 'apostle' or 'missionary.'[1] As Paul notes:

> Christ redeemed us from the curse of the law by becoming a curse for us … so that in Christ Jesus the blessing of Abraham might come to the Gentiles, so that we might receive the promised Spirit through faith. (Gal. 3:13-14)

These words point us to the great turning point in the story of the divine mission. It did not begin with the coming of Christ, but his coming and incarnation constituted the key part of the story. His death, resurrection and ascension and subsequent giving of the Holy Spirit internationalized the message of salvation preserved

---

[1] In Hebrews 3:1 Jesus is described as God's *apostolos*. 'Apostle' is simply the Greek-derived form of the Latin-derived word 'missionary' (apostle from the Greek verb, *apostellō* 'I send'; missionary from the Latin verb, *mitto*, 'I send').

previously in one nation. No longer is the temple in Jerusalem, and the daily and yearly sacrificial system required. For everything pictured in the Old Testament rituals, personalities and sacrifices has been realized in Jesus. He is God's final temple just as he is God's final sacrifice. Forgiveness comes through him. We receive every spiritual blessing in him through the ministry of the Spirit, and no longer through what takes place in Jerusalem. The Day of Pentecost and the outpouring of the Spirit on 'all flesh' (= 'all people groups') signifies the beginning of a new era of international mission to the whole world. Thus Jesus commanded his faithful apostles:

> And Jesus came and said to them, 'All authority in heaven and on earth has been given to me. Go therefore and make disciples of all nations, baptizing them in the name of the Father and of the Son and of the Holy Spirit, teaching them to observe all that I have commanded you. And behold, I am with you always, to the end of the age.' (Matt. 28:18 20)

This is a truly remarkable statement. Jesus had earlier said that he would build his church through Peter—the leader of the apostles. As if that was not surprising enough he now makes an even more extraordinary statement. Only eleven of the original twelve apostles are left. They could muster another few hundred or so in addition to their own family members (Acts 1:15; 1 Cor. 15:6). Yet Jesus is telling them 'Go and make disciples *of all nations*'! If five loaves and two fish seemed precious little food with which to feed five thousand, eleven apostles are surely too few to spread the good news among the teeming multitudes of the earth, not to mention travel the vast distances from Jerusalem to reach them. Not only so, but Matthew's immediately preceding comment is that 'some doubted.' There were eleven (Matt. 28:16); 'some' means at least three (we never say 'some' when we mean 'two'). So here we are with only eleven men, at least three of whom have misgivings, and Jesus is telling them to take the gospel to the ends of the earth! To do this they themselves will have to travel widely, and write up for widespread distribution and explanation the gospel message about Jesus.[1]

But what is just as remarkable is the extent to which the apostles were humbly obedient to Jesus' command. The fact that the gospel has reached you is testimony to that.

But do Jesus' words spoken to these eleven men have any bearing on the life of the church today? We do not automatically assume that everything in Scripture is directly addressed to us, do we? After all, Jesus was speaking to them, not to us; we were not present on the mountain in Galilee. In fact we were not even born. So we cannot simply assume that this command speaks to us in the same way it did to the apostles. After all, most of us 'stay' rather than 'go.' And we do not assume that everything Jesus said to people applies directly to us (his words in Matt. 19:21 serve as an illustration. Few Christians imagine 'Go, sell what you possess and give to the poor' applies to them in the same way it did to the rich young ruler).

It helps if we read Jesus' words in their original context. He is making a series of universal statements:

(1) Jesus now possesses *all authority in heaven and on earth*;

(2) The apostles are to go and make disciples of *all nations*;

(3) The apostles are to teach those who come to faith *'all that I have commanded you'*; and,

(4) The apostles are given Jesus' assurance that he will be with them *for all time*, to the end of the age.

This fourfold statement explains why the command to take the gospel to all the nations is an ongoing responsibility for the church. Being a 'world Christian' is not an optional extra.

---

[1] Throughout the Farewell Discourse in John 13–17 it is evident that Jesus is preparing them to do this. See John 14:26; 15:26.

First, Jesus claims to possess all authority in heaven and on earth.

We need to set these words of Jesus in their full biblical context. At creation, God gave Adam and Eve all authority on earth to establish his kingdom. But they forfeited it to Satan through their sin. This is why Jesus refers to him as 'the prince of this world' (John 12:31; 14:30; 16:11 KJV). It is also the reason why, in Jesus' wilderness temptations, he was able to make a *bona fide* offer to him of 'all the kingdoms of this world' if Jesus would simply bow down and worship him (Matt. 4:8, 9).

The reason this was a real temptation was because it was precisely the kingdoms of this world that Christ had come into the world to win back. But he had come to do that through his death and resurrection—not by sinning but by dying for our sin; not by bowing to Satan but by overcoming him. It is against this background that on the cross Jesus 'disarmed the rulers and authorities and put them to open shame, by triumphing over them' (Col. 2:15). Now not only is all authority in heaven his as the eternal Son of God, but as the Son of Man he has regained authority on earth:

> … to him was given dominion and glory and a kingdom,
> that all people and languages should serve him;
> his dominion is an everlasting dominion,
>   which shall not pass away,
> and his kingdom is one
>   that shall not be destroyed. (Dan. 7:14)

Sometimes today it is claimed that the great missionary movements of the eighteenth and nineteenth centuries destroyed the native culture of the people to whom the gospel was brought. Missionaries of the Colonial period are often decried as ravaging other peoples for the prosperity of their own nations.

The truth is a diameter apart from this. Granted missionaries are imperfect. But the fact is they were by no means always welcomed by those whose goal was empire expansion and personal gain. But since missionaries went in the name of Jesus Christ, they knew that part of their goal was to see the transformation of all cultures into the kingdom of God.

In this connection I recall an intriguing interview with two missionaries in Vanuatu (formerly the New Hebrides). They decried to the young interviewer the way early missionaries had despoiled the native culture. But he knew more about the history of Vanuatu than they expected and replied with a further question: 'But am I not right in thinking that before the missionaries came the natives here were cannibals and actually killed and ate people? Wasn't that their culture?' There was no reply. There could be none, for the young interviewer was absolutely right. The truth about King Jesus had saved these people from paganism and self-destruction. It came to them when they were like the Gadarene demoniac, beyond human control. But the gospel had wonderfully saved and transformed them.[1]

The motive for missions remains unchanged since the first days of the Christian church. All authority on earth belongs to Jesus. But not all on earth bow to Jesus. So long as that is true it will also be true that the church is under obligation to take the gospel to all the nations.

But, we may say, it was specifically *the apostles*—not us—who were told to do this. True, but remember what Jesus said they were to do: '… *teaching them* to obey all that I have *commanded you*.' And part of what Jesus commanded them, which in turn they were to teach others, was to 'go and make disciples of all nations.' The responsibility given to the apostles by Jesus was to be passed on to every succeeding generation of Christians. So the command is no less real and urgent today than it was on the day Jesus ascended to the right hand of his Father.

---

[1] For a gripping account see *John G. Paton, Missionary to the New Hebrides*, ed. James Paton (1898, repr. London: Banner of Truth Trust, 1965).

At a famous meeting in 1786 at which William Carey spoke about the importance and urgency of taking the gospel to the ends of the earth, an older minister John Ryland Sr said to him: 'Young man, sit down! When God pleases to convert the heathen he will do it without your aid or mine.'

Thankfully Carey saw that this view of things confused God's power with his purpose. Of course God can convert people without using missionaries; but he has chosen not to! Instead he planned to use men and women like ourselves, and to give us the privilege of bringing good news to a lost and dying world.

As we do so, he has promised to be with us. When we go into the world to tell people about Christ he is with us. The command to the church to take the gospel to the nations is co-extensive with the promise of Jesus to be with us as we do ('and behold, I am with you always, to the end of the age'). As David Livingstone believed, this is the promise of a gentleman and he has never failed to keep it.

There was a time, not so long ago, when children in our churches were encouraged to think of missionaries as the great heroes of the faith; it was the aspiration of many parents that perhaps the Lord would call one of their children to serve him where the gospel had never been heard or where it was little known. The children were taught that God can call any one of us to serve him, and that normal Christian discipleship—normal church membership—is to be willing to go anywhere and to do anything the Lord requires of us. Obedience is the only way to maximize your life for Jesus Christ.

We hear less talk of that kind today. Are there fewer Christians who see themselves as committed to going anywhere to do anything Christ wants? But this is in fact the calling of every member. In one form or another we are called to fulfil the great commission.

What then does obedience to the great commission mean for those of us who remain in our home church all our lives? The commandment is still ours to obey even if we ourselves do not physically leave our homelands. We hold the ropes for those who go. We love them, pray for them, support them materially as a church family. We write to them sharing our news and asking for theirs. We welcome them and care and provide for them whenever they have opportunity to return home for a season. We get to know them and to sense increasingly that we share together in the same bundle of life and in the same divine mission.

When I was sixteen I attended a conference for boys who were thinking about going into the ministry. One of the speakers was a missionary from Seoni in South India. I cannot now remember the details of our first conversation but somehow I had his address and wrote to him, and he replied; and so for a number of years, until he and his wife returned home, I had the privilege of a correspondence with a man whose shoes laces I did not feel worthy to tie. It was typical of him that later in life he would come to hear me preach. I learned from him what a missionary is at heart—a humble servant of Jesus Christ, the King, obeying him in the ongoing task of establishing his kingdom throughout the earth—wherever he calls us to be.

At the end of the day this is what it means to belong to a church:

• to be part of a fellowship that worships and serves locally, but whose vision stretches to the ends of the earth and to the end of history;

• to be part of the family of Christ in which brothers and sisters are united in faith and hope and love.

It is the greatest privilege in the world to believe in Christ and to belong to his people.

That is what being *devoted to God's church* is all about.